DONNA LONG

finding my **Wings**

The story of an abusive childhood and
the courageous battle to overcome it

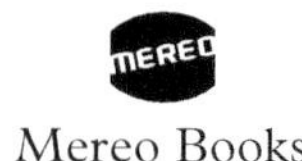

Mereo Books

2nd Floor, 6-8 Dyer Street, Cirencester, Gloucestershire, GL7 2PF
An imprint of Memoirs Books. www.mereobooks.com
and www.memoirsbooks.co.uk

Finding My Wings
ISBN: 978-1-86151-992-4

First published in Great Britain in 2022
by Mereo Books, an imprint of Memoirs Books.

The address for Memoirs Books can be
found at www.mereobooks.com

Mereo Books Ltd. Reg. No. 12157152

Typeset in 11/17pt Plantin
by Wiltshire Associates.
Printed and bound in Great Britain

To my late husband, Bill, who was always by my side. He gave me
years and years of love and understanding. He showed me a world of
kindness and acceptance.

PREFACE

If every person could reveal their deepest fear, I think it would be the fear of rejection. When a child is not loved, rejection seeps deep into their soul. Rejected children carry a lifetime of sorrow. Sometimes it's also a lifetime of guilt, anger and low self-esteem. I was one of those children – totally uncared for and without the security of someone who loved me.

Finding My Wings is a personal story of the struggle of a very insightful little girl who had the courage to stand alone and just say NO. It unfolds from the earliest years when she was dependent on others and unfortunately controlled by their ignorance, their power and their own personal needs. Then the story goes through the pain, the fear, the neglect and the abuse that are often consequences of living in a dysfunctional family. We become aware of the continual struggle and predictability of future events caused from a background without education, without love and without any kind of security.

This story is not about a small part of my life. It is a story that continues throughout my adulthood, how I started life and how I worked to change it.

Actually the book isn't just about me. It's about the pain that so many hold onto throughout their lives. This story is about the cry for the recognition that we all need and the cry for justice that few of us ever get. Unfortunately this is a common story in all too many homes in the world. In short, my story is the universal need to be heard.

CONTENTS

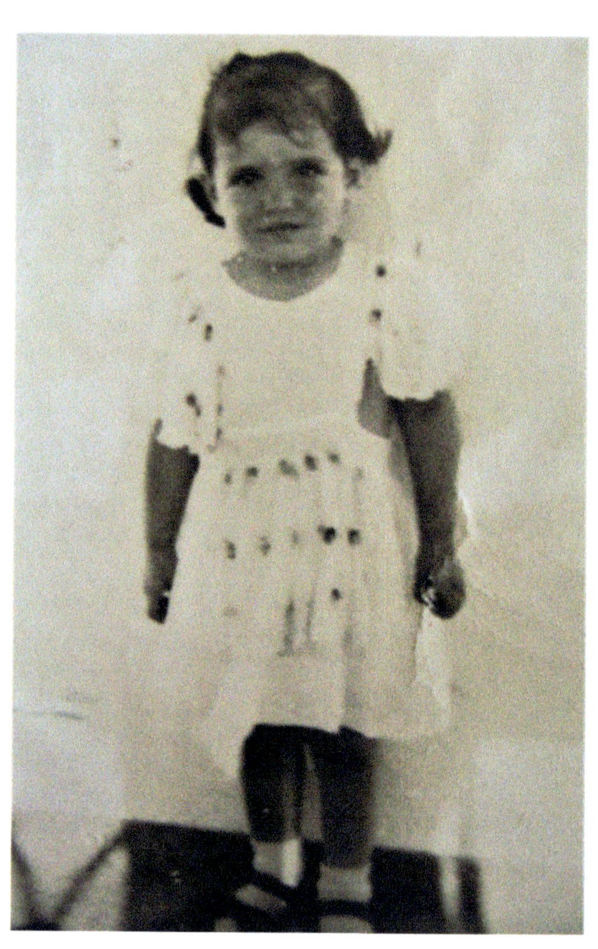

INTRODUCTION

In the first few years of my life, I suspect my mom and my real father had their own problems, which started the abuse and the negligence towards me from my family that continued for most of my life. Later my stepfather came on the scene and everything went further downhill from there.

My whole childhood and family life were severely dysfunctional. Every day and every thing was chaotic. My parents were too absorbed in their own struggles to have any desire, or time, to teach a child the basic things they might need to understand in order to grow up and learn to love or succeed in life. There were no boundaries on physical or mental abuse. Actually there were no boundaries on anything. There certainly wasn't any compassion or concern about education, the environment, animals or anything else that lived or died. We simply existed and were each on our own to survive.

We grew up in a world surrounded by secrets: secrets about rape, incest, physical violence, verbal abuse, explosive tempers, hatred, jealousy, drugs, depression, ignorance, alcoholism, infidelity, vindictiveness, manipulation, fanaticism, rage, blame, denial, emotional deprivation and for the lack of a few more seconds, even suicide and murder. These were a part of our daily lives. Each word describes an emotional scar on the soul of a child which penetrates the rest of its life. And in my family, we lived with all of them.

When children are surrounded by these conditions, it's what they see and learn. They usually continue the cycle of dysfunction when they themselves grow up; it's what they know. The result is that their children, and sometimes even the next generation too, usually struggle most of their lives, never breaking the cycle. This has indeed continued with most of my grown brothers and sisters to this day.

Unfortunately, this is a common reality. Bright little souls are extinguished each and every day for lack of seeing another way to live. In my home, it was a struggle just to survive. And all I wanted to ever do was to get away from it as fast as I could. Even as a seven-year-old, I knew that I was different from the rest of my family. I always watched things around me and in my mind, I questioned everything. I wanted to know the answers to all the secrets. I purposely began to distance myself from my family. I knew I didn't fit in and that I wanted a different reality. It felt as if I never really had been a part of 'my' family. I just existed in my surroundings, waiting for my chance to leave. I watched from outside and instinctively knew that to survive, I had to shield myself from the life of what I saw every day.

Much of my younger years I really don't remember at all, except for some of the abuse. I remember that in full detail. But from the time when I was seven to thirteen, I have forgotten almost all of my childhood. I forgot where I went to school, where I lived, who I knew, and if I was ever happy about anything. I do remember asking questions about things, when we were 'little'. But somehow I never did get any answers from mom or dad. I quickly learned not to ask anymore. And so my past became even more of a mystery. Who was I, and what happened during all those years in our house? I wanted to know WHY I still feel tremors inside of me when I think of dad. And why I could hardly look at his eyes, even in a picture. Why didn't we have any family functions or go anywhere or ever have relatives visit us? Why weren't we in any school activities, and for that matter, why couldn't we go outside and play with friends?

When I was 16, I left home and immediately started to collect all the facts that I could about my childhood. I searched out relatives and asked if they knew anything about those early years. I found old neighbours and asked if they had any information they could give me. I searched out relatives and asked if they knew anything about those early years. I asked my brothers and sisters what they remembered. They each seemed to remember more than I did. Some didn't want to bring up the past. But I got enough from their own stories to help me put together the pieces, and I began to write this book. And the more I uncovered about my childhood, the more I wanted to write about it, to write about my feelings and the strength it takes to cope with life when you start with nothing but fear and hate.

This is a story about choices and change. At first I wanted to title my book 'Unending Fear', because that's what my life was. Then I decided to call it 'me me', the only words I ever spoke until I was almost three years old - Mom said no one ever knew what I wanted because all I would do is rock back and forth and say 'me me'. Looking back, I think I was trying to say 'feed me, love me, take care of me'. Of course, it wouldn't have mattered if they had understood what I was saying. Mom and dad were totally preoccupied with themselves and unprepared to take care of their children. Later, at the suggestion of my editor I decided to title it 'Finding My Wings'.

It is only now, in later life, that I have the knowledge and understanding of how my past had continued to affect my whole life. Finding My Wings has given me the information and the strength to continue to fight against every kind of abuse. I hope that sharing my story will be helpful to others who have lived in similar circumstances. We all have the responsibility to ourselves and our own children to break the cycle of abuse and not become victims.

PART ONE

Chapter 1

Indelible Imprints

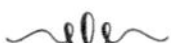

Both mom and dad came from totally dysfunctional families of their own. Mom's family came from Italy. They brought with them lives of verbal assaults and daily beatings. They had the old country ideals where the man was total lord and the mother was worshiped, but at the same time expected to stay in her place. There were four children in her family. The oldest daughter had a child in her teens, out of wedlock. For this 'disgrace' she was beaten so badly that she ended up in hospital for over a week. It was then rumored that the father of the baby was her very own father (later this was found out to be true). The second oldest child, and only son in the family, said he was beaten every day of his life when he was young. For the most part, he became the same tyrannical father as his own father. Neither of his two children speaks to him anymore.

The next daughter left home at the age of sixteen. She totally renounced her family at that time and has never made contact with them ever again. Some 30 years later, my mom looked her up and found out that she had created a whole new 'fantasy' life as that of an orphan. To this day, I don't think her husband or children know anything of her past life.

Mom was the youngest in her family. She was born with kidney trouble and was in and out of hospital most of her childhood. She was a sickly child and maybe because of that, she was spoiled and treated as a very special child.

We never were around any of our relatives very much. I still don't know anything about my real father. I never have seen a picture of him, and I never could find out any information about him, other than mom once saying that I looked like him. I only know that he left mom when I was about three. My attitude now is that he must have been pretty smart to do so. Anyway, my stepfather came on the scene when I was about four. I never could get any real details about his family background, but what I have heard through the years is steeped in a history of maladjusted personalities.

My father's family sounded worse even than mom's. There were five children. Their mother died when they were all young, leaving his father to bring them up alone. He did it with the use of force, and followed it up with threats and guns.

My stepfather was number three in his family. A one-sentence description of him is that he was a pedophile who took a pathological delight in being mean. His older brother was also sexually perverse. I only met him once or twice when he was around the age of 40. Even then he thought it was funny to take out his penis and tell lewd jokes. One of dad's sisters was called the 'weird one', whatever that means. I never met her. The other sister seemed nice the few times I remember meeting her. She is married and seems to have a normal family life. I wrote to her and told her that I was writing this book. I asked her if she would give me some information on her family's background – she never answered.

Our family story begins when mom got married the first time. She was eighteen, and she brought to her marriage her own abusive background. She was insecure, totally narcissistic and without self-esteem. She lived only for the love of 'her man' at the time. She married and quickly had three children. Margaret is the oldest, born in 1944. I came next, in 1945. My brother Tony was next, born one year later in 1946. We three were born in Brooklyn, New York.

I can make an educated guess that both mom and dad were totally unprepared for married life or the responsibility of raising a family. It didn't seem to matter that dad had a low level job, or that mom didn't work at all. It didn't seem to matter that neither had dreams or goals for their future. They were in love and they immediately proved it by having children. I think they were more liberal than most at that time and obviously less responsible. Mom told the story of how they used to hide marijuana in the baseboards of their apartment, and how they went out a lot and had a good time. I don't remember any of this, but mom never was one to give up much of what she wanted just because they didn't have money, or they might have children to feed.

Margaret was the first child and was very wanted. Oh, the stories and pictures we have of Margaret! She was loved by both mom and dad and remained the most special.

Six months later, mom was pregnant again, with me, and she was sick all the time. She told the story of how she was always tired, that her marriage was not happy anymore and she didn't want to have another baby. She used to think it was funny to tell me how much she hadn't wanted to have me. She totally hated having any part of that pregnancy. Nine months later, a name wasn't even considered for me. None. She was given gas during labor and didn't even know I was born.

I was pulled out with forceps during delivery. My bald head was misshapen, my face was swollen and my body all bruised. Mom laughed every time she told the story that when the nurses brought me to her, her first comment was that I was the ugliest baby she ever had ever seen. The nurses pleaded, 'Oh no, she's beautiful, look at her pretty eyes', but still there was no maternal bond. She definitely didn't want me. To this day, on my birth certificate it only says 'BABY GIRL'. The nurses took it upon themselves to name me, so I was sent home with the name Donna Marie.

Life for mom and dad must have been full marital misery by this time. Dad didn't even pick mom up at the hospital. My aunt, who used to live with them for a while, said that they fought all the time, even physically sometimes. That must have been the beginning of why mom always seemed to resent me most of her life. But even an unwanted child and an unhappy marriage didn't stop mom from getting pregnant again. And only one year later, my brother Tony was born.

A world of stress and hardship can be more predicable than the weather. Life is hard when you start out with nothing and then keep having children to make your life even harder. And it just gets worse when you never accept responsibility or learn from your mistakes.

I'm sure it got worse every day until they finally decided to get a divorce. I was two or three years old at the time. The courts gave custody of us three children to mom. The story goes that one day before the divorce was final, dad just left the house and took 'his beautiful daughter' with him. He kidnapped Margaret and left the state and planned on keeping her with him in hiding. So whether to find her child or get even with dad, Mom left and went to find Margaret and bring her back. She liked to tell the details of how she had to plot and plan to 'steal' her back, how it took her months and months to find them and how dad wasn't ever going to give her back. Mom was gone a long time, but when she came back, she did have Margaret. And no one ever heard from dad again.

There are no pictures and I have never had any information about my birth father's full name. Whenever I asked questions about him, mom would say he was a worthless hippie, or just a drifter, or sometimes she said he was a poet. And she said he looked like me. She always claimed he was Italian, but I couldn't trust what mom said or even if she really knew. My aunt said he was Jewish. Most people I have been told me that the name—Scodes—has a Greek sound. Who knows? I only knew that dad was quite a lot older than mom. And by the time I was old enough to look him up, the records showed he was dead.

The rest of what I found out about the time when mom was gone was that Tony and I were left 'with some neighbor' until she came back. And when she did come back, we three children were left again with several other people and/or would be handed off at different locations. We never could get answers from mom about who we stayed with or exactly why. The bits and pieces I have put together about this are something like: Your mother was always out having a good time. No one was ever with you children.

Margaret remembers us being sent to some sort of orphanage. She said she cried and cried because we were separated and she didn't know where her brother and sister were. Tony remembers being put in a closet with me crying the whole time. I don't remember anything. It was already my way of learning to survive. Another time I was told that I was left with a lady who kept me 'for a while' and that the lady then took mom to court to try and adopt me. Another story is that a neighbor turned mom in to the social services for neglecting her children. That was a time when few ever did such things – it wasn't usually even considered.

Our aunt says that Tony was only three months old and had to be taken to the hospital for pneumonia and that all of us were 'always dirty and neck high in piss'. I have only one picture of myself during that time. It's the picture on the cover of this book. I look like I am about two years old. I'm standing alone in a rag doll dress and both of my fists are clenched. I have deep, deep questioning eyes. It's not a picture of a happy little girl. She looks lonely and afraid.

But I understand now that I was always a smart little girl. I learned very fast how to take care of myself. Mom often told the story of how Tony was slow at learning to walk, and then one day she knew why. She said she saw me biting his legs when he tried to stand up. She said Tony would pull himself up and try to stand and then I would bite his legs so that he fell down. When he dropped his bottle, I would take it and drink the rest of the milk. Mom said she never could tell what I would do next. She said only Margaret could tell what I wanted.

Looking back at these stories, it's pretty obvious that there was no consideration for the physical or emotional needs of any of us. I see those years as a time of total abandonment. As I reflect on the early lives of those three little children, I see Margaret as already taking responsibility of caring for her younger brother and sister. I see myself as a very strong survivor who already knew how to get what I needed. And I see Tony already associating pain with any effort to succeed. The consequences of an unstable beginning were already apparent.

But none of that mattered to mom, because she was once again busy looking for a new man to love her and take care of her. She was always out having a good time. No one seems to know what happened during the next few years, except that we moved a lot.

Mom met our new 'father' when I was around four. He was a tall, slender young man, almost six feet five inches tall. He was handsome and only 24 years old when they got married. Mom was 25 and already had three children. I have to assume that they might have been happy the first few years, although mom never told any stories about wedded bliss.

There would be four more children added to our family by my stepfather. Seven children in all, four girls and three boys. Ever since I can remember, everyone in the family just wanted to grow up and get out of the house as soon as possible. None has a continuing relationship with the rest of the family.

I have listed each of my brothers and sisters below in chronological order with the date and place of their birth.

Margaret—1944, Brooklyn, New York

Donna—1945, Brooklyn

Tony—1946, Brooklyn

Charlene—1950, New Jersey

Joye—1952, Puerto Rico

Charlie Jr.—1954, Puerto Rico

Paul – 1956, Key West, Florida

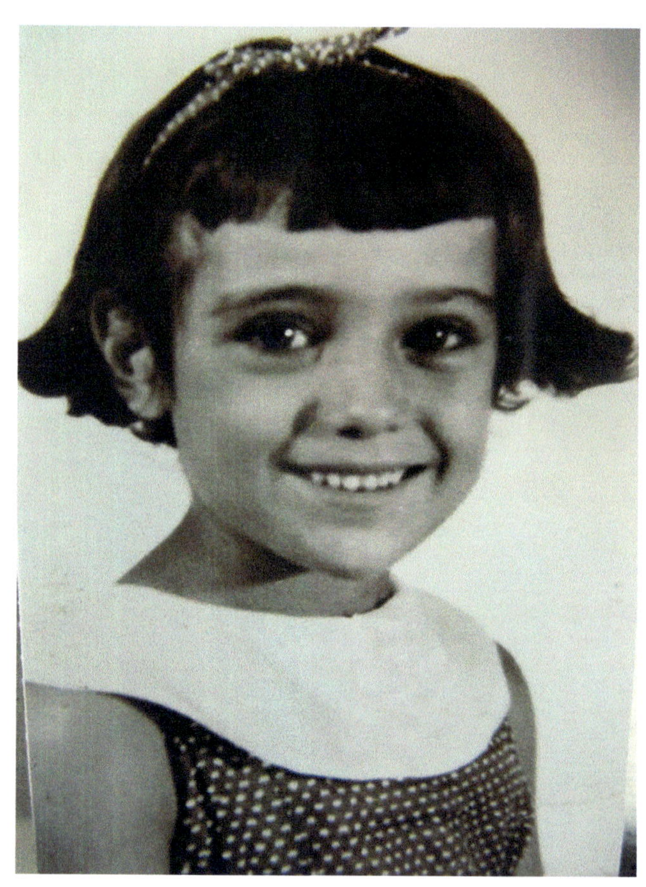

Chapter 2

Vanishing Sunshine

~elle~

My first real memory with our new father was when I was around five years old. I remember we all went on a trip to the circus one day. This was a big outing, and we called our new stepfather 'daddy'. We have a family photo that shows me holding a doll on a stick. We all had happy faces in that picture. And I remember that doll. It had feathers on it and I remember dad getting it for me, even though it cost a lot of money. Daddy really liked me – he called me 'Sunshine'. That made me feel very special. I loved that name and I loved the circus. SUNSHINE. It was wonderful, but it quickly faded, and the fun times didn't last very long.

Mom got pregnant again, and this time she had to go to the hospital for a long time. It was another one of those times when we three older children were sent away. This time we went to our Aunt Vera's on our father's side of the family. We had never met our Aunt Vera but we were told that dad couldn't take care of us while he worked, and that mom was in the hospital. So Aunt Vera would take care of us – for a while.

We were told that we were going to take an airplane ride – alone. That was in 1950. There weren't many people flying on airplanes in those days, let alone such young children traveling 'unaccompanied'. We were told to hold hands and be good. The story was often told of how cute we looked with our names and destination pinned onto each of us. Margaret was six, I was five, and Tony was only four years old.

I remember it wasn't a surprise that we were going to be sent away. I suspect that we already were quite flexible about being sent to different places. And I was excited about flying on an airplane. I remember that I got to look out the window. How ironic that that very experience might have stored away roots which would later become part of my future.

Anyway, as I was told, we stayed with our aunt for three months, or longer. I don't remember anything about the visit except that it was strange to sit down at a table for dinner. And I remember wondering what the red bottle of ketchup on the table was. Tony said 'it looks like blood' and I kicked him under the table and whispered to him to be good or they wouldn't let us stay there. Looking back on that memory, I wonder – why did Tony immediately connect the color of red to blood? And why did I already know that if we weren't 'good', we'd be sent away?

When we did come back home to mom and dad, we had a new sister. Her name was Charlene. She was born very premature and weighed only two pounds eleven ounces. It was written up in the paper that it was a miracle that she had survived at such a low birth weight. Born so small in 1950, she surely must have been a fighter.

It quickly became MY job to take care of her most of the time. I was taught how to fold a diaper, pin it together and be very careful that I didn't stab the baby with the diaper pins. I took great care and put my hand under the cloth so that if I did stick the pin in too hard, it wouldn't hurt my tiny baby sister. I liked the job of being the mommy to her. It came naturally and was very easy for me having her with me most of the time, but Charlene also cried a lot. And once she fell off a chair where I had put her. And then I remember--I really still can see it happening-- the time I dropped her on her head. It really sounded hard and she was screaming so much that she couldn't breathe. She cried for a long time and I knew I was in trouble. I could hear dad running in and yelling, 'what happened'? I don't know what happened after that except that I couldn't move. I was petrified – literally scared stiff.

It seemed like Tony was always getting into trouble too. He stuttered. He still wet his bed. He was only about four when I remember dad getting real mad at him because he had wet his bed again the night before. Dad made him take off the bed sheets and bring them into the bathroom and put them in the tub. Tony had to bring them in one at a time, walk right past dad, and with each step he had to point and say, 'That is my bed, that is the bathroom'. And when he put each sheet in the tub, he would get slammed and told to go get the next one. After everything was in the tub, Tony was shoved in with the sheets and told not to get out until they were all washed.

I watched and I remember thinking right then that dad looked almost happy being so mean. I knew he didn't care what he was doing to Tony. I knew he deliberately wanted to put the fear of God into him and I could see the fear in Tony's eyes as he wobbled past dad each time. And I could see the meanness in dad's eyes. I was scared just watching when he was so mad. But no one else seemed to notice or care what was happening.

That memory is most painful to me. After that, I didn't like my daddy anymore. Our emotional or physical needs were never considered. And no one seemed to learn that stuttering and bed wetting are common effects of emotional trauma. No one cared that it could affect a child for the rest of his life.

We moved to Puerto Rico a year or so later. It was a warm

climate there and I remember all of us kids played outside the house without shoes or tops on. I had a friend there and I remember putting little flowers all around our shorts and in our hair. I think it was a happy summer before I actually started school.

My sister Joye was born in there in 1952. Then my brother Charlie was born two years later, in 1954. I remember being outside a lot, even if it was while taking care of my younger brother and sisters. But then something really changed in our house. We weren't allowed to go outside and play or allowed to even have friends anymore. Mom stayed on the sofa almost every day—sick. Margaret and I were in charge of everything. We took care of our younger sisters and baby brother. We made the baby formula and cleaned dirty diapers. We cleaned the house, washed the clothes, and even stood on a chair outside to hang up the clothes and take them down. We also helped mom with the cooking and cleaning. Tony still stuttered and wet the bed.

I don't remember exactly when it was or how old I was when the sexual abuse started. I think I was around six or seven. We all went to a Catholic school and I remember learning in first grade all about how much Jesus loved everyone. And one day when I was playing on a swing, I remember I was singing the song 'Jesus Loves Me This I Know'. I can still see myself swinging and singing, 'YES Jesus loves me, YES Jesus loves me, for the bible tells us so'. But I remember that even as a young child, I questioned that. Did Jesus really love… me? Just because the 'bible tells me so?' And if Jesus loved me so much, why did he let my daddy be so mean? And why didn't my daddy call me Sunshine anymore? I didn't know why I didn't believe what I was being told. Or why I was starting to get angry at everything. And although I have a smile on my face in my first grade picture, behind my eyes I see a very serious little girl.

Around second grade I remember learning from church that God didn't let little Jewish children get into heaven. 'Because they weren't baptized'; they had to suffer in purgatory forevermore because their parents didn't have them baptized. Only baptism would take their sins away and only then did children get to go into heaven. I didn't understand that at age eight, and I still don't. But right then and there, I decided that I didn't like God anymore either. Oh I know, the church has changed its story now. But how could anyone have ever thought that not letting children into heaven was the command of a loving God?

I realized from the very beginning that our family was different from others and that I was different too. That I was always afraid of something and that every single day was filled with fear - fear of knowing that someone would be beaten. Someone would be thrown into a wall, or picked up by their hair, or one of us would be punched in the face or thrown down the stairs. Or maybe just told how worthless we were or that we could all 'rot in hell'. Sometimes it was just a look. A look that said, 'tonight you're going to get it'. Tonight it's YOUR turn and I'm coming into the room. It simply was the way things were. We accepted it. It had become our everyday way of living, and it never stopped. It just got worse.

I shared a room with my sister Margaret. My feeling is that dad came into our room almost every night of our lives. I was never surprised when he came to our bed. I just didn't know if it was going to be me or her, this time. Once I woke to hear Margaret fighting with dad. I asked her if she was okay, and dad punched me in the stomach and told me to mind my own business. Another time I remember all too well, because it was different. He had me sit up and then pushed my head down onto his penis. I remember trying to lift my head away, but he was pushing my head down really hard. And as I fought, he pushed me down even harder. I remember that I was choking and I couldn't breathe. And the next day my mouth hurt.

I don't really know if it happened more often with me or with Margaret, or for that matter, what he actually did some of the times when he came into our beds. And I don't know if I usually ever fought him or even said no. But I fully expect dad was quite active with both of us, probably about the same time he stopped calling me Sunshine. Actually I don't remember dad ever threatening us not to tell anyone about what was happening. He didn't have to tell us. His looks told us he would kill us. And his violent temper explosions said 'you're next'. But what I remember most in all those years, is that I was NEVER asleep when he came in. I always saw him coming.

Even though I knew it wasn't 'right', I quickly learned to just accept things as they were and keep quiet. My instincts told me to keep it a secret. It was survival and just another part of the struggle to stay alive. But how often did you come into our room, dad? Why wasn't I ever surprised by it? How many times was it done that I don't remember at all? And is this when you started to blame ME for your own miserable sins?

We moved again, this time to Key West, Florida. Mom was still always sick or going to the hospital and sure enough, pregnant again. Our brother Paul was born in 1956.

In our case Margaret and I did talk about it a lot to each other. We saw it happening to each other in the same room that we shared, and we both decided together not to tell mom. We said she would just cry or leave dad, and then we'd really be poor. But we also both agreed that mom probably had to know already. How could dad sneak out of bed every night without mom knowing he was gone? I never did understand that. It still fascinates me as I hear stories of other children who were molested, that so few of them ever tell anyone. How well I know the reasons why.

One morning when we were all in school, someone came on the intercom and asked that Margaret, Donna and Tony report to the principal's office immediately. There, we were given instructions to go straight home. No reason was given and we didn't ask any questions. We just walked home as fast as we could, each of us wondering if something horrible had happened to mom, or to the baby.

Dad was waiting for us when we got home. He picked me up by my neck and showed me the dust on top of the door sill. He told us we didn't clean the house good enough! And he made each of us start all over again – to do our job again. This time the right way. Mom always had 'excuses' why she couldn't help us. She was always sick, or tired. Or she was usually mad at us too for some reason. I didn't know exactly what was happening or why, but I knew right then that I didn't like my mom anymore either.

I don't remember mom ever trying to stop dad from being so hard on us. She seldom stepped in to say a kind word or help us in any way. She just didn't interfere. I knew that dad was dangerous and out of control. I asked her once if she could make him stop beating us. All she said was that we probably deserved it. Once I remember sitting outside on top of a metal garbage can and crying. I was maybe eight or nine years old. I knew more about God now and I asked him why. Why couldn't someone help us? But I instinctively knew that there was no answer to my question. Nothing was going to change.

There was always chaos around the house and I just tried to stay out of sight. I was becoming more and more distant from everyone in my family. I often didn't know what was happening to my brothers and sisters. Someone was always in trouble. Someone was always bleeding or having to go to the hospital. Mom was always 'sick'. I just did what I was told as fast as I could and got out of the way. It was definitely safer. I tried to get outside any chance I could. I would always volunteer to go to the store for mom or take my baby brother or sister out for a carriage ride, to just be quiet and try to disappear.

But I did love to go to school. School was a whole day AWAY from home. I liked most of my subjects and I had some nice teachers, even though some weren't so nice. I remember once being in a Christmas play. I was going to be an angel – even if I had never seen one with black hair. It was really a big deal to me to be an angel and I couldn't wait to go to school and have my wings attached. The teacher that was helping me commented that my hair was always such a mess. She tried to comb my hair and asked me if I ever combed it at home. I remember thinking how odd that question was to me. NO, I was nine years old and I don't ever remember combing my hair.

But I was definitely a strong young girl and I always had the most fun in physical education. I was very active and excelled in every sport I tried. Oh, I never wanted to miss a day of school. Luckily I was very healthy too. I never got sick. I never even had the chicken pox, the measles or the mumps. But come to think of it, we weren't allowed to get sick. That's all there was to it.

Mom was in the hospital again this time, she was *really* sick. She never seemed to get up off the couch. She was always complaining about all her aches and pains. We actually started making fun of her. And I started to become aware that I had no sympathy for people who didn't try to help themselves.

All the while we—Margaret and I—had more work to do. Mom stopped being able to help at all. There were eight loads of wash each day and ironing to do too – ironing that mounted and filled a whole closet. Groceries were ours to put away. Cooking dinner usually became my job. Cleaning the whole house was a daily chore and we all learned quickly how to do it right. Basic living needs never stopped. All the responsibilities of raising a family were on the shoulders of my sister and me. Everything was excessive with such a large family and it was overwhelming. We never had time to think that childhood was anything but HARD.

Not even school. Most supplies we needed were out of the question. I was embarrassed because I constantly had to borrow paper, and whenever I did get some of my own, I faithfully returned what I owed to others, so then I quickly once again had none left for myself. I failed a sewing class because no one would take me to the store to buy a zipper for the skirt I was making. Putting in the zipper counted for 50% of the grade. I didn't have one. But by now, I had started not to care anyway. We just did as we were told, period. And there was no time for anything else. Actually around this time, I think I just stopped being able to think at all. I was just existing, without being conscious of having any feelings at all.

When I was around thirteen years old, I got sores around my chest. No one knew what they were and mom didn't give it much attention, until it got worse and started to spread. We finally went to see a doctor and he told mom it was the shingles. He said shingles was caused by a virus that cause painful eruptions on the skin and that this usually happened when the immune system is weakened by such events as emotional stress, severe illness and/or aging. He also told mom that it was rare to see them in children.

But mom had more important problems to think about – herself. She was now always crying or angry at dad. I asked her once, 'Why don't you just leave him'? And she said it was because she had seven children and no job. She said because 'I love him'. I think it was about this time that I realized that mom didn't have to accept such a hard life. She was a part of the problem. She and dad could have made different choices, but they didn't. We children paid the price and took the brunt of their misery.

At age fourteen, I remember everything being in full swing. Mom and dad were always fighting, sometimes violently. Dad was always having an affair. Mom was always finding out and crying about it. I was always fighting with Margaret about who did more work in the house. Tony was always running away and getting into trouble. Everyone was always making fun of Charlene, the cry baby. The younger kids were always hitting each other, being yelled at and getting into trouble at school. When tempers flared, anything could happen. We were punched, thrown, or chased. And when we were caught we were beaten with anything in dad's hands at the time. And a punch wasn't just one punch. It became a pummeling until someone was a bloody pulp.

I had long hair and remember wanting to cut it so dad couldn't catch me by my pony tail so easily. Dad's favorite way to punish me was to grab my pony tail and then fling me into a wall. Once I was hit in the face with a baseball bat at full force. I remember spinning around and falling to the ground, and actually seeing stars. When you get hit like that, you really do see stars! I don't know if they're always in color, but mine were. But even though it hurt an awful lot, we never went to the hospital to have it checked. We never went to the hospital anymore, because doctors might ask questions.

The pain in my jaw finally went away and it was only years and years later that I learned from an X-ray that my jaw had been fractured.

Dad was just plain mean, and we were all terrified of him. Everything started to become more and more out of control. We weren't allowed to go outside for any reason. We were seldom allowed to even do our homework, as the work in the house took priority and had all our time and attention. Needless to say we never were allowed to participate in after-school activities, never allowed to have friends over and couldn't talk to the neighbors. Obviously none of us ever went to a birthday party or even got gifts when our own birthday came around. Vacations were only for rich people. We just would come straight home every day and face the wrath of my father. We had never been out to a movie or to any kind of community event. We never stayed over a friend's house, had company, went to a wedding or a funeral, church or even a fast food place for dinner. The whole family was just falling deeper and deeper into an uncontrollable cycle of fear, abuse and anger.

It was around this time that I remember wanting to just grow up and leave the house as soon as possible. I had to take control of my future. I felt a new strength and an insight that allowed me to take charge of my own life and know that I could change it.

One day dad came home especially upset and this time he threw the whole dinner table across the room. Food was everywhere, even on top of the curtain rods and our clothes were a mess. Of course it was left for us to clean everything. When my clothes started to dry they also started to get hard. I wondered why and quickly figured out it came from the sugar in the tea. And that's when I realized that I could use sugar water to starch my crinoline when I wore a flared skirt. It worked! I remember smiling and thinking that I had learned something from this. I began to look at everything in my life as a way to learn new things. I was thankful because I was beginning to understand cause and effect. And I knew that I could learn to make things work with what I had. Not always the way I would have wanted to learn, but absolutely knew right then and there, that some day, some day, I would have a better life.

School was almost over. I never looked forward to the end of the school year. Things just got worse during summertime; we didn't have school to protect us. And then when school did start again, we always had the same first assignment: write an essay about what you did over summer break. I listened as other kids in class read about their vacations, their fun times playing at the beach, their families being together in a park. No, it wasn't the same for us. It's hard to imagine now how socially shut off from the outside world we were. But by now I didn't focus on the bad things. I tried to make the most of what I had. I knew that some day I would have my chance at a better life.

This too was a certain kind of self-protection. And it served me well through the years. I purposely looked for any good I could find in the world around me. I still do; I believe we have choices and I was making sure I made the best ones I possibly could.

We moved again. Now we were in San Diego and dad found new hunting grounds for more sexual affairs. Mom was again finding out about the affairs and crying like she was going to die. She always asked one of us to help her in some way while she plotted ways to get back at him: 'gouge his eyes out', or 'Kill him'. Once in a while she would kick him out of the house, only to let him back a week later, meaner than ever. I started to understand how insecure mom was and how she never learned anything from her mistakes. She remained a victim of all her problems.

And now she was pregnant – again! I was fourteen and very embarrassed that mom was still having kids. I remember learning in school about the population explosion and I asked her, why do you want more children? And she said, 'Because I am Catholic and we don't believe in birth control'. And besides, she said: 'I love babies.' All I remember thinking is, What? She must be kidding. She never took care of any of them. Why did she always just want more children?

Of course, mom was very sick with her pregnancy. She had

only one kidney and it was deteriorating rapidly. As a result of this condition, the fetus was slowly being poisoned by the toxins in her body. A few days after the birth of her eighth child, the baby died. We never did see the little girl but I remember thinking she was lucky. Lucky she didn't have to grow up in our family. When mom came home from the hospital, I could tell that she was very depressed, probably more so than usual, but we weren't allowed to talk about it or ask any questions.

Chapter 3

Unending Fear

~elle~

As young teenagers we became virtual slaves to our parents. I was the one who tried to blend in with the background, just do as I was told and stay out of sight as much as possible. Every day brought a new level of hurt and hate. Even the dog had learned to go and hide when dad came home.

Dad was always mad for some reason and ready to take it out on anything or anyone in his way. One time it was me again. He came after me and took me into the bathroom and closed the door. He put his hands around my neck and started to choke me. His hands went completely around my skinny neck and clinched with super strength. I couldn't breathe. I fought to move his hands but he lifted me high up over the toilet, choking me as hard as he could. I must have weighed all of 85 pounds, and I just dangled from his six foot five inch height. I remember flailing and fighting and gasping a lot, and then I must have passed out. I don't know for how long.

When I woke up, I was seated on the toilet and dad was supporting me at my shoulder. At first I didn't know what had happened and then dad asked me if I wanted some water. When he went to get it, I fell over. He grabbed me and I remember thinking that was nice of him. I do remember noticing that he was as white as a ghost. He looked scared and I wondered, was he scared because he knew he had almost killed me? How close I was to dying? How long was I unconscious? Did he have to breathe for me so I would regain consciousness?

You son of a bitch. I was petrified of you and sucked the life out of everything you touched. But I was so used to emotional and physical abuse that I thought he was nice to give me water. I said thank you.

Of course, nothing got better. It seemed to me that dad actually looked for more ways to be mean. One time one of our cats had kittens. We were told immediately that we couldn't keep them. Dad told us he was going to drown them all. Then he made sure that I watched as he strangled one of those tiny kittens 'to put him out of his misery'. I remember his smile as he saw me watching him when he did this.

Once he told Tony to clean up the dog poop in the yard. When Tony said there was nothing he could pick it up with, dad told him to use his hands. And then he pushed his hands into the mess and laughed as he watched Tony picking it up. Dad actually liked being mean.

And that's when I realized that some people are simply evil. They have no desire to question what they do or take time to consider its consequences. I'm sure they never give a thought to the emotional or physical hurt it causes others. Period. Dad was a pedophile and a pathologically cruel person. Both mom and dad were so unhappy that nothing else mattered to them. They lived on each other's misery.

Soon everything was back to survival mode. Any minute someone would be beaten. Someone would be bleeding. Dad was kicking or punching everything around him. Once I saw him punching something in a corner. It was so bloody and beaten so badly that I couldn't tell if it was a human or an animal. Later I found out it was Tony. And many, many years later I found out that Dad had been a small-time professional boxer and had been awarded a golden glove award. He was a professional boxer and knew exactly what he was doing! He didn't give a damn. He just took advantage of his power to hit harder.

By now all of us kids were programmed to wake up and start working. We didn't stop for breakfast, left for school without lunches and no, I never remember combing my hair or even brushing my teeth. Most of the places we lived had warm climates, so we never wore much more than a pair of shorts – no shoes or tops. Although I was quite skinny and undeveloped at fourteen, I was beginning to notice that boys were looking at me. When dad noticed it, he took action to extinguish any hope I had for newfound attention.

One day dad told me to go out and get the groceries from the car. I didn't have a top on at the time and asked if I could go to get dressed first. He said, 'NO!' and literally kicked me out the door. There were some neighbor boys outside and I was horrified as they heard the door slam and saw me tumble outside. I could tell they were looking at me and I had to walk right in front of them with nothing over my chest.

I had started babysitting by then and was making a little bit of money. I didn't own a bra. I didn't really need one yet, but I wanted one, so I asked if I could go buy one. Of course most of my money went directly to mom. But I did get to buy one and once I had one, I never wanted to take it off. I wore it to school and after school and I even wore it to bed. It never dawned on me that it was dirty and should be washed.

I was growing up now and more keenly watching the part mom played in all of this. I began to see how her own insecurity caused never to want to take responsibility. How she loved being a victim and always blamed someone else for all her problems. Mom never looked at herself to learn from her mistakes. And she never seemed to realize that she was a part of her problems and had the power within herself to change. But it was very clear to me. I knew. I never said a word. But mom and dad must have seen my insight and how I didn't accept what they were doing, and I became the scapegoat in my family. Dad took special delight in finding any new way he could to embarrass me.

One day, I remember that dad had a friend over—maybe a man about 30. The man commented that I was growing up to be a pretty girl. Dad said, 'Yes, but she's filthy. You should see her bra'. Then he looked right at me and smiled. He meant to humiliate me to the fullest extent. I remember just looking back at him with no response at all. I had already learned it was easier not to have feelings. Yes, I knew my bra was filthy. I just didn't know what to do about it. It never dawned on me that I could wash it out overnight and still have it on the next day. Anyway, I didn't have time to think. I was just existing and now I was beginning to lose my self-confidence. I was simply finding it harder and harder to understand or get a hold of my feelings.

So now we were three teenagers in the house with four younger brothers and sisters, all out of control and wanting something different. Dad was away more and more. That was good news to me, but with him being away so was most of the paycheck. I remember us being quite poor. Food was scarce. We had to wait for Tony to come home from mowing a lawn in hopes to have some money to buy dinner. Dinners were usually pasta creations or beans or rice with vegetables. We never did have a hunk of meat. Needless to say, we never had soft drinks or desserts either. I don't know if there was any kind of public assistance at that time or if mom just didn't know how to ask for it, or if she didn't care enough to even notice, but we simply did without a lot of food and basic needs.

During those years I didn't eat much anyway. With seven kids in the house, any food we did have was eaten within minutes of being put on the table. Once I remember going over to a friend's house before school to wait for the bus. She was still eating her breakfast even though it was time for the bus to come any minute. I remember thinking how strange that was to me. Who ever had time to eat breakfast? Or who had time to make lunch and take it to school? Making lunch or having money was out of the question for us, so I usually just did without. I was used to not eating. Nothing was affordable and nothing had any value anymore, so it didn't matter.

I even started to fail some classes. Inside, I knew I was losing control. I knew I was slipping down. Down somewhere bad. How could it be that we were so emotionally starved, physically beaten and sexually abused and NO ONE noticed it? And no one stopped it either? Surely someone could have seen this happening. How could it be that nothing ever changed?

Around this time, I had started making more money and had a few steady jobs baby sitting or helping someone clean their house. Although all of us were expected to give our money to mom, a few times I was allowed to keep some of it and usually I chose to buy milk at the school cafeteria. One day the nun behind the counter told me that I should get more to eat because I was so thin. She said she was going to 'pray for me'. I think she did and someone listened. Today I am not so skinny.

But time just continued to pass and after the days there were always the nights. When dad was home, he would sometimes come into our room and just stand at our bedroom door, smoking a cigarette and just looking at us. I trembled inside just seeing him there. Was he deciding who to choose later in the night? Other times I remember waking up with wet sloppy kisses all over my legs.

But then it stopped. I don't remember any more sexual abuse for almost a year.

Margaret was now 15, while I was 14. She was a beautiful young girl and much more developed than I ever was. She had a figure that most can only dream of having. I remember thinking she was more like a typical teenager than I was. She loved music and boys. She always liked to have fun. She always complained if she didn't like something and she seldom wanted to do her share of the work around the house. Mom's answer to this was for me to do even more of the work rather than listen to Margaret whine.

That's when I began to see myself as the Cinderella of the house. At one point I never even had a place to sit at the dinner table because there weren't enough chairs. Sometimes there were nine of us eating and only eight chairs, so I sat on the floor in a corner to eat. It didn't matter. I was always too busy working anyway. I began to accept my position in the family. It's just the way it was.

One time when dad was gone for a long time, my mother's sister came to visit us and she noticed the way mom favored Margaret. She said, 'Why does Donna have to do everything'? 'All I ever hear is Donna do this, Donna do that'. Mom said she made me do it because I never argued. Later Aunt Dolly must have said something further about this to mom, because they argued and then, mom never spoke to her again. I don't really know what it was all about, but mom never spoke to her sister again for 30 years.

Then dad came back. He seemed a little bit different. For

some reason, he didn't come into our room as much anymore. Margaret and I immediately thought it was because he must have started molesting our younger sisters.

That was when we decided to had to tell mom. We wanted to try and protect our younger sisters and we had to stop dad. I don't remember what mom said when we told her. I don't remember her reaction at that exact time. I don't know if she believed us or not. But that night after we went to bed, there was a big loud fight in the kitchen and I do remember that fight. Mom had a knife in her hand and was screaming and crying that these were her 'babies'. Yea right – her babies. She said she was going to report dad to the police.

And sure enough, the next day, we were all taken to the police station. There we were put into a room and had to tell our story of what happened. I was horrified and embarrassed as a young man heard everything we said and did. And then he said we had to write it all down. And I had to ask that same man, 'How do you spell the word 'penis'?

Some time shortly after that, I guess when mom found out what was going to happen to dad, she quickly decided not to go through with the charge. She changed her mind! She told us to tell the men that we were lying and that we had made the whole story up. It's unimaginable how a parent could do this to a child. I remember one of the men saying to her, 'Mrs. Gertz, please don't do this to your daughters'. But mom didn't care about us and insisted it was all a lie. We said the same thing and all the charges were dropped.

On the way home mom told us that from now on we were going to forget everything and be nice to dad. She also said that we should go to confession because what had happened to us was a sin. She said WE had sinned and had to go to confession. Then she told us that when we went to confession we should not tell the priest it was dad.

I remember that confession very clearly. I can almost see myself and hear every word I was saying. I was scared to death and my knees were actually trembling. I didn't know what words to use or how to explain what happened, let alone talk to a priest about it. I was terrified that the priest would ask me WHO did it.

I entered, knelt down and started the Act of Contrition. My voice cracked and I felt sick. I was fourteen years old, but my voice changed into the squeaky sound of a little girl. I remember using words like 'peepee'. Actually I don't remember every word of that confession. Or anything else of what I said. I just finished and remember looking back and seeing the priest look out of his confessional at me. I said my penance and left. As I reflect back now on that time, I know that I had emotionally reverted back to the vulnerable little six-year-girl old that was still inside me.

We moved again, this time to Virginia. Dad now had two jobs and was gone a lot. Mom started going out with a man named Bernie. She fell in love with him. She would ask me help her fix her hair up all fancy when she was going out to meet him. And I had to zip her up in her always too-tight dresses. It was the new routine every night that dad worked late.

Once I asked her why she didn't get a divorce and marry this man. She said because he was Catholic and getting a divorce was against the religion. This religion was becoming a good excuse for everything, and none of it made any sense to me. How could someone practice only the part of a religion that they wanted to believe, while the rest was totally ignored?

Anyway mom was really in love. It became a long-term affair but then one day it simply ended. Mom stayed in her bed for days and days. I had never seen such a deep depression or such big, suicidal tears. I asked her if I could help her. I got on my knees by her bed and held her hand. I told her that I didn't know what to do to help her. I told her that we all loved her and needed her.

Two days later, I told her that there wasn't anything in the refrigerator for me to make for dinner. And she said, 'I don't care', and told me to go away. In my heart, all I could think of was that surely she knew that her seven children were more important than Bernie. But no, she didn't even think of her children. Mom came first, her man was next and our needs came last. And right then I stopped ever feeling sorry for her ever again. Mom was just in her own world, only thinking about herself.

By this time, I was babysitting for some regular costumers who called me back every week. Most of the time the husband drove me home. I didn't like it when the men would offer to drive me home. I quickly learned that a lot of men were creeps. At least half of those husbands would make some sort of pass at me. Not bold passes – they were sneaky, subtle little passes. Like when they would slow the car down to a mere crawl and look over at me and tell me I was pretty. Or one would put his hand on my thigh and tell me he liked to drive me home. My insides would just tremble. I never trusted any man.

School was different now too. I used to think I was smart, but now in High School, I wasn't passing a lot of my classes. Everything seemed to be getting harder. I even noticed that I looked different from most of the other kids. I had long black hair and wore dangling earrings. This was long before it was fashionable, and only minorities or hoodlums wore long earrings. I began to drift towards the troublemaker side of the class. I never really felt like I belonged there, but then I didn't fit in with the smart kids either. I didn't have time for friends anyway.

And that's when I failed the ninth grade. Margaret failed the tenth grade. By this time, Tony had failed almost all of his grades. He was not even going to school after fourth grade.

I remember really being embarrassed about failing my class. I always liked thinking I was smart, but now I wasn't sure anymore. I didn't know what was really happening at that time. I just felt unconnected with everything around me and I didn't know how to pull myself together or change things.

I was in the ninth grade – second time around – when I met my first real friend. Her name was Jackie. The timing was perfect. Jackie became the one person in my life who helped me with what I needed most. She was a role model for what I wanted to be someday. She was soft-spoken and smart. She was rich and made straight As. Her mother made her lunches that she brought to school. She wore beautiful clothes too. Jackie looked like a porcelain doll. She had beautiful red hair, white smooth skin and was delicate in all her actions. We were about as different as any two girls could be both inside and out, but Jackie accepted me right away and we became fast friends. Jackie was the first person who really made a positive difference in my life. We didn't have much in common, but somehow I gave her something she needed and surely she gave me my first chance at life. I still thank her for that. Our friendship has lasted to this day – over 55 years!

Jackie and I had a great bond. We shared our homework projects. It was particularly hard for me to learn to study because I simply didn't know how to do it. I had forgotten much of my earlier confidence and felt lost, but I knew that if I wanted to change my life, I was the one who had to do it. This friendship gave me the opportunity.

Jackie helped me understand how to take tests, and she taught me how to study for them. With her help I went from remedial English and other slow classes to getting a high C average in my freshman year. Then I got Bs and Cs in my sophomore year, and then I actually got on the honor roll in my junior year. I focused on getting good grades. I wanted to go on to college and have a better life. Not needing a man was my first priority. And not being poor was a close second.

On the home front, all of us started getting phone calls, and the telephone became the new reason for dad to go into a rage. The phone was torn out of the wall more often than it was attached. But I was going forward. I was now getting attention from the teachers, the sports teams and even the boys, and I liked that. I liked being smart and I was finding a lot of new reasons to smile. I don't remember ever doing young and foolish things. Even at sweet sixteen, I never went into boy crazes or had time to listen to music. Certainly I didn't have time to hang out with friends or go places with them, but I was definitely attracting attention and boys were asking me out on dates.

There didn't seem to be any reason why I couldn't go out at night, but dad usually said 'NO'. Once or twice when I was allowed a date, mom would make me cancel it at the last minute and tell me to stay home. I never understood why, and I felt sorry for the boy who came to pick me up for a date and then was told to just go home. Sometimes dad had his gun by his side. No one ever argued.

Then, almost as if it was planned to stop me in my tracks, mom said we were going to move again. I had just finished my junior year. I knew it might hurt my chance of graduating if I left now and it was critical to me that I stay and finish my senior year. I desperately wanted to graduate. I just couldn't move!

So I asked mom if I could stay behind in Virginia. I told her I could stay with her friend Ida. I could get a job and pay Ida for my room and board. I would also work for her in her house. Mom asked Ida, and she said okay. So I took one suitcase and moved in with this dear lady.

My sister Margaret was already pregnant and given her only option at the time – get married and leave the house. So that's what she did, and they moved into a trailer park. I thought my brother Tony had gone along with mom and dad. I didn't see him for many years. Later I found out that he had started off with mom and dad, but at some distance away, he was told to get out of the car. He was told to get out in the middle of nowhere and to leave. He was told he was old enough to take care of himself. They just drove away and left him.

Although Tony was now almost 15, he had no self-esteem, no education and no place to live. He had been called 'animal' most of his life. Mom and dad gave him no more thought than they would give an animal, just like the name they always called him. Of all the abuses I have seen in my childhood, Tony's emotional and physical abuse touches my heart the most.

But I didn't know any of that at the time and I was in my own world of new-found freedom. I discovered that I really liked living with Ida. She was always good to me. I remember the first time I tried to help her clean the kitchen floor, I got down on my hands and knees to scrub it. She screamed for me to get up. She said I didn't need to do that. Ida liked me and treated me with kindness.

I started to work at a grocery store, and my life continued to blossom. Everything was different. Boys were looking at me everywhere I went. I had my own money. I bought a beautiful dress and went to the prom. I learned to dance. Oh, how I loved to dance! I especially liked the polka, when the man would lift me right off the floor and twirl me around and around. I felt pretty and had a lot of boys trying to date me. I felt comfortable with Ida and her husband.

Soon Ida wanted me to marry her son, Noel. He was a soft-speaking young man. He was good to and me and genuinely kind. Noel was my first romantic boyfriend.

But now I was discovering something even more interesting about my new world: boys were ridiculous around young girls. And if you were blessed by being pretty, they would do almost anything you asked of them. I quickly learned that I had a great power. It didn't matter to me if my boyfriend was going to be a 'steady' or just a one-time date, I took this new power and I used it. Although I never asked for much and seldom got gifts or fancy things, I did expect dinner. If the man couldn't afford to feed me, I usually didn't accept a date with him. I definitely wanted to be fed.

During this time, Jackie and I had a great time growing up together. I don't know why we actually became such good friends. Maybe it was my desire to be just like her. Maybe it was because I chose her to be on my sport teams when no one else would. She never could catch a ball. Or maybe it was because deep inside, we both knew that each of us had a very special gift to give the other.

I graduated on the honor roll in my senior year. I know it doesn't sound like such a big deal to a lot of people, but to me I saw my whole life changing. I was gaining self-worth and confidence in myself and everything I did now began to make a difference.

This was the time when I literally danced myself through life. My smile and my body and my brain became the promise of my future. I wanted to go to college and I had decided that I would like to become a physical education teacher. I wanted to work with girls at the senior high level. I noticed that that was an age when most of them stopped wanting to play physical sports. Back in the early 60s, most girls weren't into sports yet. But this was where I excelled. I was athletic, capable and strong. I loved being active. And still, I definitely felt feminine.

I didn't understand the real value of staying fit at that time. I just loved 'playing' all kinds of sports. Once again, this natural desire gave me another direction that would remain a priority for the rest of my life.

I got into a junior college, but had to move away from Ida's house because it was too far and there wasn't any public transportation from where she lived, so I moved in with my sister and her husband while I went to school and worked full time. I paid them while I lived there. Her husband promised he would drive me to and from work – if I paid for the gas. Her husband was very controlling. He was way over his head with a wife and child and all the usual responsibilities. He didn't let Margaret go anywhere or buy anything, not even a pack of cigarettes, without first asking him. And if he did let her buy something, she had to be sure to bring back any change from the money he gave her. They had a terrible marriage from the very beginning. Her husband didn't keep his word about driving me to work and it became more and more of a problem living there. He was controlling and always wanted to be the boss. There was constant arguing between him and my sister. I stayed less than a year before moving away.

By now Jackie had moved away for her own college years. Although we kept in touch, I felt very alone and I was struggling. It was difficult finding a place to live that I could afford. I temporarily found a place at the local YWCA. It was close to public transportation but unfortunately, even at that time, it was in a terrible part of town. Here I was once again introduced to the slimy side of life. It was all around me – filth, ignorance, perverts, indecent exposure and poverty.

Once while I was waiting for my bus, I noticed a man come and stand very close behind me. I was reading a book and didn't stop to really look at him, but since my eyes were down, I noticed his shoes. They were old and worn. I felt sorry for him. But when I lifted my head, I saw that he was exposing himself. Luckily the bus came and I quickly got on and never looked back. I was terrified. I felt an old anger grip me and the familiar fear of being vulnerable again.

At work, I called the police and reported it. The police promised they would come by the same bus stop the next morning and be watching for this man. They told me that they would be hiding and that if I saw the man, I was to 'point him out' and that they would get him. So the next day I was ready to do as I was told. I was watching carefully for any man who walked towards me. I didn't know who I was actually looking for but then I saw a man from a long distance coming in my direction. I watched him as he walked closer and closer with each step. He was very handsome, not more than 30. He walked right up to me and I stared right into his eyes, but I didn't recognize him.

Then I looked down – and saw the same shoes I had seen the day before. Even though I almost passed out, I stepped aside and boldly pointed at him. The man just stared at me with a confused look, and of course, no policemen came to my rescue. But the bus did. I called the police the minute I got to work and asked where they were. They said they hadn't come and were sorry. I couldn't believe that the police were never there. They lied to me! My mistrust of men grew stronger that day.

This pervert knew where I caught the bus. He seemed to know my schedule. And now he probably knew I was trying to put him in jail. I was terrified. I called the police again. I was furious that they had promised to be there to help me and hadn't been. I told them I had been left alone, pointing at the man. How could they?

This time the police promised to come again to meet me

before I went to the bus stop. They drove me around in the car, hoping that we might see this guy again and try to catch him the next day. And we did – we found him. I pointed him out and the police stopped the car and ran after him. They caught him and I had to go to court to press charges and formally identify the man. He was sentenced right then and there and got three months in jail.

After it was over, I left the courtroom feeling somewhat satisfied. Then, as I was getting into the elevator, the man I had just put in jail walked right into the same elevator with me. He had been immediately released on bail. No one bothered to tell me, or explain how the system worked and that this might happen. I was alone with this man in the elevator. He stood close enough behind me that I could hear him breathe. He was close enough to slit my throat. My whole body literally shook with fear. I didn't understand how it could have happened, but after that, I learned another real good lesson. The courts couldn't be trusted either.

And I had to find another place to live. I couldn't stay in that part of town, so again I was looking for a place I could afford that was close to work. This time I found a room with a family who lived close to where I worked. They rented out a room to me.

I was there for about two months when the husband of the house came into my bedroom. It was the middle of the night, but I was somehow awake and I saw him as he entered the room – smoking. Everything seemed to happen in slow motion. He sat on my bed and asked me if I ever got lonely. I was calm and really not surprised at all. I just looked at him for a long time and then I said, 'get out of here or I'll call your wife'. He hesitated a while, but then left.

The next morning there was cigarette ash by my bedroom door. And the next week his wife came to me and asked me to leave. She said her husband thought I shouldn't stay any longer because they needed the extra room. Yeah, I'll bet he thought that. Like, 'get her away before she tells my filthy little secret'. Actually I was ready to go anyway. But where? Where was there a safe place?

After telling an older lady I worked with that I needed a place to live, she told me I could stay with her for a while. She had a daughter about my age and she said we could share a room. So I moved in with her. They were all nice to me while I lived there. Everyone laughed and we all had dinner together. Her daughter and I got along very well. I felt like I was welcomed as a part of their family.

I was almost eighteen now and had hopes of getting an apartment of my own as soon as I could afford it. And of course I still wanted to get a degree and maybe go into teaching physical education. But I quickly found out that I needed to take a lot of courses in biology and anatomy. That was hard for me. I didn't have the background in education for those kinds of advanced classes. I didn't have the money for all the college courses I needed. And I didn't have time to study when I was working a full-time job. I was just getting by. Once again, my life began to slip out of my control. That was the year that John Kennedy was shot. 1963.

Everything was coming down on me. Completely alone, I needed to find another way to make my life turn around. I was still in school but already trying to find other ways to make things happen, just in case I couldn't do it in school. Marriage was the usual answer. I had met a few good men – just a few. I knew it was possible to meet someone good and I began to place myself right where I would meet the most eligible of them all – I did all my homework in the nearby medical library. I read at the tennis courts. I joined the debating team. All around me were 'desired husbands to be'. The men who asked me out were all educated and had high income potential. It was easy and almost fun. I felt like candy attracting the flies right to me.

Now that I had these educated men asking me out, I quickly found out that I was definitely out of my element with a few of them. Some I dated had a vocabulary far above my own. One took me to my first symphony and said something about the conductor not having a 'score'. I didn't understand what he meant and said something stupid like, 'I thought he was good'. Others took me home to meet their parents, who immediately wanted to know more about my background. I learned quickly. I grabbed onto every new thing that came my way. Although always coming from behind, I felt that I was going forward again with my life.

Once I had a first date with 'Mr. Rich and Handsome'. We went to dinner and then out to a movie. On the way home, he stopped the car and made a sexual pass at me. I resisted. He tried harder. I resisted harder. Then he got angry and pushed me away from him. He pushed me so hard that I hit the opposite car door. He said he might as well take me home right then. I whispered yes, he should. Luckily for me, he did. I remember not being angry about that. But I knew something had changed in me at that moment. A quiet new determination was brewing inside me. I would never allow myself to be pushed around, not by anyone, ever again.

Then one day I came home and saw that the lady I was living with, my happy family mother, was crying. I went over to her and asked what happened. Her face was all swollen and bruised. She said, 'Johnny hit me again'. I had never seen that side of her husband. She said her husband had a temper, sometimes. And she said he sometimes 'slapped her around' when he got mad. I almost couldn't believe it. I really couldn't. All I could think was that every man in the world must be a fucking abuser. God, I can hardly write about this anymore. It was all around me. It never went away. Even today as I have distanced myself far from it, it still affects me. I continue to see it everywhere.

That incident made me feel vulnerable again. Once again, it was getting harder at school and it seemed like every time I got up, there was something to knock me back down. That was a time when I remember I had some kind of out-of-body experience. I could actually feel myself floating up, and then I could see myself as I was looking back. I saw a young girl in the parking lot carrying books. I could tell she was trying to blend in with the other kids. She was trying to be a part of the social crowd – trying to be like the other kids. But I could tell she didn't belong there. It wasn't her reality. She was out of place and just acting the part. She was just existing. She was totally unconnected to the pleasure of being alive. I could actually see it. And I felt sorry for her.

Finally, I moved out and got my own apartment and for the first time was really on my own. Everything came down on me fast – the rent, the transportation, the job, the school. I had no support from anyone and I was definitely struggling to cope with it all. I knew I just had to keep going forward and do what I had to do to stay strong. I don't know how I managed. I just did.

Then one day I met an older man who asked me out on a date. He was thirty-five years old or so. I dated him a few times and liked him. He said he worked for a major airline and asked me if I would like to be a stewardess. I had never even considered being a stewardess. To me that was like being a movie star! In 1965 it was indeed a very desirable job to have. But it was in a world I knew absolutely nothing about. I had never been on an airplane except that time when I was five years old. I had never traveled or even finished my education. He said that he could get me an interview any time I wanted it. I asked if it paid well and if he thought I could get the job without a college education. He said he thought I would be perfect for it just the way I was.

I really wanted to finish college, but I did think about that job idea. I knew I'd probably like being a stewardess. Sounded like a great opportunity to me. So I thought, sure. If they really did hire me, I could quit school and join the airlines. I came home, gave it a bit more thought made my decision. I said YES.

He said he'd bring me a ticket and I could fly to Chicago the next day for my interview. And that's just what happened. I went for the interview and was accepted. I got my wings in January of 1966. I was based in Chicago and my life opened up to a brand new world. It was filled with exciting new experiences, new opportunities and an unbelievable amount of new freedom. I was twenty years old and it was one of the best decisions I ever made in my entire life.

PART TWO

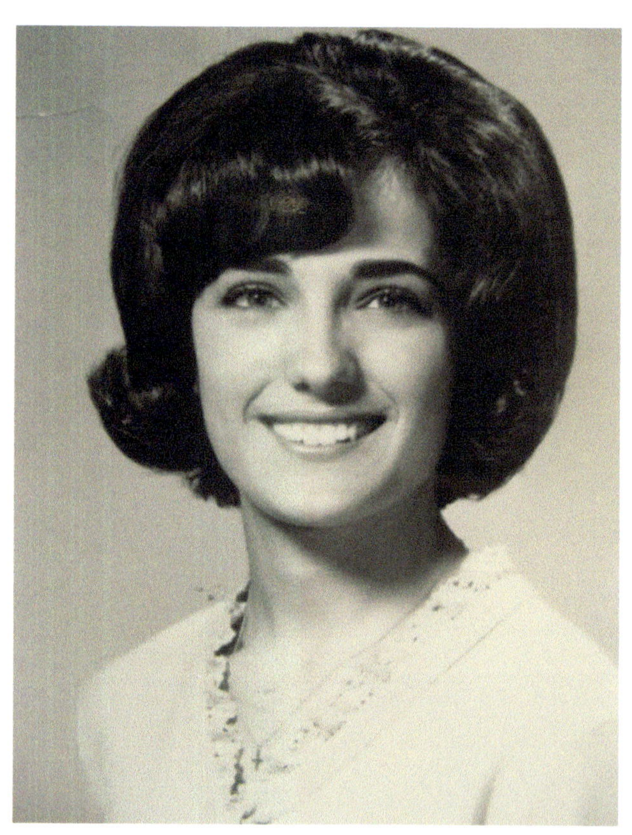

Chapter 4

Blue Skies

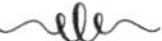

What an explosion! I literally flew into a new life. I was totally on my own now and had enough money to get a decent apartment. I was stationed in Chicago and found it to be a fascinating city full of adventure around ever corner. This was the life! Everything was new and everything was exciting to me. Being a stewardess (that's what we were called back then) opened the doors to a wide world of everything for me. And I wasn't about to miss anything or be left out from any of the opportunities coming my way.

One of my first flights was a non stop trip to San Francisco. I knew the minute I got off the plane that this was where I wanted to live. Six months later, when I could put in for a domicile change, I did just that and moved to the beautiful city by the bay.

San Francisco was the ultimate. I got an apartment in the Marina close to the Golden Gate Bridge and Palace of Fine Arts. Every hillside view sent my heart into a flutter. Every building, large or small, was filled with unique wonders of architecture, food, smells, color and sounds. And the cable cars really did seem like they reached halfway to the stars. People were freer in their attitudes and actions. They seemed happier. The sky was always blue and the breeze was cool.

I loved everything about San Francisco. My flights coming home always made me smile. I loved flying and was discovering the vast differences of many new cities, all with a special quality to call their own.

Most passengers who flew in those days had professional careers. It wasn't far from my mind that it also gave me the bonus of putting me in the right position to meet good potential husbands. My new selections could be from pilots, actors, professors, lawyers, doctors and politicians. Back then, many years ago, being a good stewardess meant actually sitting down and talking to the passengers. It was a part of our job. Most of us were always being asked out. We were often given small gifts, getting invitations to shows or invitations to dinner while we were on layovers. I met all kinds of interesting people and learned new things from each and every one that I met. It was never hard work to me and never hard for me to start up a conversation either. It all came naturally.

I must say though that I was still thinking of my future and I was selective in husband hunting. I always checked out the first-class passengers, and usually found someone listening to the classical music channel. Without ever knowing why, I loved the glorious sound of the opera, and now it was an opening for conversation and promise.

On one trip when I was flying into Washington DC, I sat down by a young man and started blabbering about the new Wolf Trap Farm Theater there. I mentioned how good the 'acoustics' were (my new word) and how I had tickets to see Beverly Sills in 'La Traviata'. Not really knowing a thing about what I was really talking about, and not really listening to his response, I missed it when he said HE would be singing there at that evening. I went on and on about how I admired Beverly Sills and couldn't wait to see the opera.

Then he asked me if I would like to meet her. I said YES without skipping a word and without hearing what he was saying. He again said HE would be singing on stage with her and could get me backstage tickets. He said all I had to do was tell security my name and say I was an invited guest.

Sad to say, I did not even know who it was I was sitting next to, but true to his word, I went backstage after the show and did as he said. I was ushered right into the dressing room of Ms. Beverly Sills herself. I don't remember much except that she said she was starving and asked if I knew of a place that might be open at this late hour. I suggested a pizza joint close by. I was dating a pilot at that time and she invited both of us to join her and the staff. We actually shared pizza together. We talked about our different lives – opera singers and theater life verses stewardesses' and pilots' lives. It was a wonderful evening with conversation on two subjects so very, very different. She was as lovely and as interesting as I had ever imagined. And she was kind enough to make me feel that I was too. It still ranks among my best memories.

Every time I met a new person I discovered another choice, another direction for the way I wanted to live my life. And I loved the traveling. Wow, layovers were the best! Every new city or town that I stayed in had its own special charm and history. Every place was a whole new adventure of something new to see or do. I never got tired of flying all over America. And I never worried about money. I always had enough for what I needed. Nothing could have been better suited for my personality. I was a vibrant young lady and I was indeed flying high. I felt true freedom and I was finally able to see myself going forward again. Everything was certainly coming up blue skies for me.

I went on my first vacation alone when I was twenty-one. I liked the thought of going to Hong Kong, which was about the most unusual faraway place I could think of at the time. I had a great desire to understand far-off cultures. And so I chose to start exploring the world of the Orient. I went all alone, and still remember that vacation very well. The very first day I arrived there, I met a whole squadron of naval flight officers who had been out to sea for several months. They had just come into Hong Kong for R&R at that time and to be honest, they were all quite ready to meet any young American girl.

We coincidentally met in the lobby of the same hotel and each of those handsome men in white uniforms didn't' skip a minute in getting their chance to come over and talk to me. They wanted to take me out for dinner and dancing and parties. Some wanted to show me the sites and take me on tours. I was definitely the 'belle' at every one of their events. I did manage to see all the tourist attractions before leaving to travel onward to Kyoto, Japan. I got the name of one particular man and promised to keep in touch with him when I got back to the states. To say the least, it was a marvelous vacation.

Most of the men in the squadron lived in San Diego, so it wasn't hard to keep in touch with the one I liked. With travel perks, I could visit as often as I liked. I kept a long distance romance going for a year or more and often heard stories about his roommate, Bill. Known by a different nickname, he was a good-looking guy who I definitely noticed. But he was also the one that actually never flirted with me at all while we were over there in Hong Kong. He was the quiet one who didn't ever seem to be interested.

Anyway, about a year later, I was told that Bill had joined Pan American Airlines and was in training to be a commercial pilot. My relationship with the other guy was ending, although we remained friends for some time. One day he called me and asked if it was okay for him to give Bill my phone number because he was out of training and got based in San Francisco. Sure it was okay with me! Yes, I said. I hung up and smiled. I waited for Bill to call.

It took almost three months of calling and leaving a number before we finally got together for a date. He was now busy flying all around the world and I was busy living to the fullest life anywhere my flights would take me. Our schedules were hit and miss at best. But once we did start to make time for each other, our dates were always pleasant. Bill was a soft-spoken man. He always took me to nice places and he always told me I was beautiful. He was a true and gentle man.

At first, our relationship was more of a friendship than a romantic affair. We really didn't have a sexual passion for each other – at least I didn't for him. This was the first time I had ever known a man—a male—as a friend. He didn't boss me around. He didn't expect sex. He didn't kiss me like he was out of control or as if he HAD to have me forever. This was very unusual and strange to me. I didn't really know what to do with Bill. But I didn't dwell on it or try to understand what was happening. He was nice and I liked being around him. That was enough for me. We both continued to date others. There were no strings attached to either of us and Bill kept coming around.

Life was busy and I was too happy now to slow down or give much thought to anything. I had lost touch with most of my family. I felt totally alone with my newfound joy and the secrets of my past. I felt secure in myself. I was starting to see that I was quite capable of doing just about anything I tried. I was flying on reserve, packing at a moment's notice, never knowing where I was going. Organizing my schedule, taking care of my responsibilities, it was all easy enough for me. Irregular schedules and long hours didn't bother me either. No fears or anxiety about going to a new place or not knowing anyone. To me it was a fun challenge. I was living for the moment. Today was all that was important. There was just so much to see and do. I looked forward to every flight and every adventure.

I was beginning to understand that my past might actually have been an asset to me in some ways. I already had the training necessary to make the best of any situation. It made me quite adaptable to change and it taught me the virtue of hard work. Both of these are valuable qualities in everyday life, but especially in my kind of job. I took it all in my stride. I had energy to spare, and my zest for life was envied by almost everybody I met. A lot of people saw me as a leader. I didn't know why, but I do think I always projected a type of confidence. Perhaps it was my quick action whenever I wanted to get things done. Or maybe just the fact that most could see I wasn't afraid to take control of things around me and just get the job done.

I always loved flying and I was totally absorbed in everything I did. My schedule gave me a lot of time off, which now gave me time to go back to school. I took night classes in Philosophy, Critical Thinking, Theology and Social Studies. I was fascinated by why people thought so differently. I wanted to know why I was so different from others in my family with the same parents and the same background. Although I went to Catholic school for eight years, six days a week, I never believed anything about the words of God in the bible. And that too made me question – why? My parents certainly never influenced me on how to believe. But from the time I entered first grade catechism, I never believed what I was being taught about religion, especially the part about babies being born with 'sin'. For that matter, I always wondered, why did anyone believe in a God at all?

I always questioned why people lived and died for words written in religious books, had words that were written by men thousands of years ago and now become gospels to their every action. Books filled with commandments and damnation and causing millions not to learn love, but to learn to fear – fear of rejection for heaven, fear of thinking for yourself, fear of questioning God, fear of judging others.

I still asked questions of the nuns, the bible scholars, the priests and theologians. They all had many answers, but none of the answers made sense to me. And finally one priest said, 'One has to believe. It all comes down to having faith'. So I looked up the word 'faith'. It means blind trust and/or without facts. Blind trust? The more I learned about other cultures and their own gods and their own bibles, the more I understood that most people needed religion because most people still lived on faith. But that wasn't for me. And the more I studied, the more I didn't believe in any of it. I had lost 'faith' a long time ago and certainly wanted more than blind trust to guide me.

During the next couple of years in school, I decided to try and regain a connection with my family. I had flight privileges, so I went home about twice a year. I obviously wasn't brought up with any close family bonds, but still I was a part of my family and even with all the chaos, I still wanted to keep in touch with them. When I did visit, I noticed that mom and dad acted like I was a danger to them. They didn't seem happy to see me and none of my brothers or sisters seemed to care that I was there. When I had left home my younger brothers and sisters were only eleven, nine, seven and five years old. They weren't taught to know anything about me. I was a stranger. They really didn't know me at all.

Oh, and there was always a 'story' when I went home. I found out that dad had left mom again when they were living in Colorado. Charlene said mom was always depressed and that she had tried to commit suicide and take all the kids with her. She had turned on the gas stove and closed up all the windows and then went to bed. Charlene said she woke up because she got really sick. She was vomiting and went over to tell mom, but mom wouldn't wake up, so Charlene went to a neighbor's house and told them she was really sick and afraid. They called the police. It was the police who took care of the kids while mom was taken to the hospital. The incident was reported as an attempted suicide. Mom says it was all an accident.

Dad must have come back after that and they all moved again, this time to Montreal, Canada. My sisters said everyone there hated them because they were 'American'. But she also said that they felt 'rich' in Canada. I wondered – what was so different up in Canada that made them feel rich? I heard they lived in a big house up there. Perhaps dad got promoted or got better pay for his International work. Or maybe it was the social system there? I don't know. Years later I found out that my brothers and sisters were in the 30th percentile in school there. But then they moved a year or so later. This time they moved to Virginia and then again, this time to Maryland.

My younger brothers and sisters were growing up themselves and didn't have much interest in anyone they had barely heard about. But I still tried to keep in touch with them. I always remembered their birthdays. I always sent Christmas gifts. I always wrote letters. No, I never got any answers back. I never even knew if they received any of the gifts I sent because no one ever took the time to let me know or say thank you.

The direction my life was taking seemed natural to me but was completely foreign to everyone else in my family. I continued to visit them through the years. I wanted to share my new world with them. I wanted to help them and let them know that there were beautiful things all around out there. Did they ever want to hear an opera or go to a symphony? Did they ever notice that some families laughed and played with their children? Did they ever want to ski or ride the rapids? Or notice that animals responded to a gentle touch? Did they ever understand that they had a choice to have a different life? No, I really never asked them that. I don't think they would have been interested. I was 'different' and to them, that meant not to be trusted. They saw my difference from them as something to fear. Their fears were nourished with a growing hostility from mom and dad that consumed them and only fired more resentment towards me. They all seemed to hate everything I said and everything I did.

I didn't know it at the time, but every time I visited them, they would talk about me when I left. They would laugh at me and attack everything about me. They called me materialistic and selfish. And the more I exposed myself, the more ammunition I gave them to use against me. There was a growing distance between us that widened more each time we were together.

I learned to be cautious about everything I said or did around my family, but this too gave them new reasons to find fault. Now my brothers and sisters acted like I was an actual enemy. So I learned stayed further and further away.

Margaret was the constant connection with me and the rest of the family news. I always did have the closest relationship with my older sister. In our conversations I was always asking WHY? Again and again I tried to understand. WHY? Why was I the center of their every problem and the cause for all their fears? I must have 'whined' to Margaret for years – almost five years of never getting the answers to that question. What did I ever do to any of them? I never asked for anything from them and never got anything my whole life from them, not even a Christmas card. Nothing. Why did they all hate me? I couldn't understand them, anymore than they could understand me. Every year I was more and more isolated from them and more distant from the world of my past.

I found out years later that mom and dad had deliberately turned all my younger brothers and sisters against me. They poisoned every sentence they ever spoke about me. They found fault in everything I said or did. My brothers and sisters blindly believed everything they were told. No one dared to question the facts or think for themselves. No one challenged the source. And to this day, that hasn't changed much for any of them.

Around this time I was taking psychology in my college studies and like everything else, I plunged myself into learning everything I could about it. I was starting to see the connections of how people think to what they do in life. I was starting to understand the answers to my own questions. My parents were desperate people, and this is exactly what desperate people do. People who are afraid, or people who are jealous, or those who have no value in themselves are the first ones to blame others. This is what they all do. They never figure it out. They blame others for their own miserable lives and they teach hatred of anything different to protect themselves from ever seeing the truth about themselves and their own reality.

Knowing this didn't help me much. It will probably always hurt me to think how very little anyone in my family cared about me or what I was doing. And it hurt that I couldn't help teach them that there was a better way to live. But it always came back to me to wonder: what made me so different from everyone else in my family? When did I learn to love reading and especially to read the classics? And when did I realize that I loved art? And when did I change from thinking ballet was boring to thinking it was sublime? And when did I recognize that the men who liked me the most were the smart ones who had ambition? I don't know. I only know that I was always aware that I wasn't like them and that I was never going back the life of my past.

My thirst for education was in everything I did. I began to

study politics. Oh I do love politics! My brain is wired to be conservative in actions, I'm critical in my thinking, which goes with a no-nonsense personality. I don't necessarily know if capitalism is the best or only working solution for all mankind, but I do think everyone has to work for what they get. In a perfect world, everyone would share the responsibility and do their part in making things better. And yes, it would be nice if everyone had an easy way of living or had things given to them when they needed them. But I absolutely don't believe it serves mankind's best interest in the long run. Without learning to take responsibility for ourselves, everyone loses. And I'm tired of helping people who don't help themselves.

The more I studied, the more I wondered if anyone can really ever change. Or is it only the circumstances that change and we just stay the same? Did I really change, or was I always this same person inside? It seems to me that I was the same person at six that I am now. The same person who knew life was a serious game about survival. I was and still am deeply sensitive to criticism, but I'm seldom insecure in my thoughts or actions. I think we are born with our personalities. I feel blessed to have been born strong and healthy and with the capacity to learn. Some people will actually never be able to do that.

I started getting New York flights and got in touch with my Aunt Dolly who lived there. She was my mom's sister. The one who stood up for me, because she said I was the underdog. She always did call me her favorite and I had layovers there, I always went to see her and we had wonderful times together. Of course mom hated me more than ever when she found out about our relationship. In her mind, I was sleeping with her enemy and forevermore would not be forgiven.

Bill and I continued to date for another year or so. Most of the dates he took me on were now centered around going to parties and lots of drinking. I guess he thought that was having a good time. Not me. I was too serious a person to think drinking had much to do with having a good time. And I didn't like Bill when he drank either. His personality changed. He had a sarcastic side and was negative when he drank too much. Whenever we disagreed, it was because I was upset over his drinking. I was still young and I didn't understand that alcohol was a powerful drug. So I allowed myself to get more and more involved with Bill. I thought that surely I could change him.

One of our biggest arguments was once when he was got stone drunk and I brought him home and he actually fell off the bed. I told him that I wanted to be more important than his bottle of scotch. I didn't think I really loved him at the time or that I would end up marrying him, but we had a bond between us and something had a strong hold on me. I felt I was needed by him and I thought that maybe I could help him. It never crossed my mind at the time that this would become another lifetime of struggle.

I didn't know anything about drugs and I never did understand why Bill had to drink. But no matter how much we argued about it and no matter what I did, he still found his answers in a bottle. He kept on apologizing afterwards, saying he didn't mean to get drunk. He kept on telling me he wouldn't do it anymore. I thought I could change him, but I kept on being pulled down with him and getting more and more angry about all of it.

I didn't know how to get out of this relationship. For some reason I needed Bill. Under it all, I knew he was such a good man. He was intelligent. He was good looking. He was kind and had a good career, and I thought, surely he would change, he would do this for me. I didn't understand my feelings for him and I certainly didn't understand his actions. During that time, I don't remember that he ever told me that he loved me. It was all very confusing to me. So I decided to try to take a break away from everything. I thought about joining the Peace Corps. I actually filled out the questionnaire and sent it to my parents for the needed reference. Of course they ignored it. Why did I ever think they would sign the papers or take time to answer the questions and send it back to me? Crazy.

I found a similar program called the Tom Dooley Foundation. This foundation offered the choice of working on a medical boat floating down the Mekong River or living in Kathmandu and working with the Tibetan refugees. We were at war with Vietnam at this time and I knew I didn't want to be on a slow boat anywhere, let alone one in the middle of a war zone. So I took a leave of absence at work and signed up to go to Kathmandu, Nepal.

Now I really didn't even know where Kathmandu was. The whole idea of going anywhere was that I was hoping that Bill would step up and save me from going to this unheard-of place. Maybe he'd say, Oh please don't go. Or, I love you, please stay and let's get married. But Bill didn't say any of those things. He said I should go and do as I wanted. If I was trying to pull out any feelings that Bill had for me, it didn't work. So at the age of 22, I found myself packing up and heading for new adventures that I could have never imagined.

Nepal is a small country about the size of California, located between the southern border of China and the northern border of India. I flew to Kathmandu by way of Hong Kong and India. The last leg of the flight was on a small parachute airplane complete with the seats on the side of the fuselage and the baggage tied down to the center of the floor and free roaming chickens in the middle. Not many tourists ever traveled to Nepal in 1968. It's surrounded by the Himalayas, and commercial air travel did not have planes equipped with the mass oxygen systems needed for passengers at such high altitudes. These mountains also stopped communications to the rest of the world. Technology had only just begun to allow access to this primitive new location.

When I finally found my way to the Foundation's Dooley House, I immediately felt right at home. I never went into culture shock and I automatically knew what to do and how to work with these humble and desperately poor people.

I started working at a Tibetan refugee camp. The Tibetans are have a very handsome mixture of Indian and Chinese features. They were simple in their wants and needs. The children walked mostly naked all day. The adults wore only a wrap made of a type of thin cheesecloth. Few wore shoes of any kind. The main part of everyone's day was spent praying, and they all had prayer wheels, all sizes of them that they spun around. It was believed that the written prayers inside the wheels would carry their prayers to God. That was smart thinking, but it didn't give them much to eat. Cows were sacred, and killing one was a capital offense. The survival rate of newborns was very low. Children were not even given names for a whole year because so few survived past their first birthday.

I worked with several other people at the Foundation, mostly international flight attendants, and we all stayed on an old Rhana estate, in a big building once occupied by a previous statesman or dignitary. But it was still without running water, heat or refrigeration. The cooking was done outside in a separate portion of the house that had an old coal make-shift stove. There were no books or newspapers to read and no paved roads or shops, but we did have one radio and we had a Jeep.

I quickly adapted to my new surroundings. I learned right away to tie a scarf around my hair so I didn't get lice. It didn't bother me to take a bath outside from a well, even if the water was very, very cold. I remember my biggest fear was that while I wasn't looking, a cow might come by and accidentally knock me into the well. I laughed at the thought and made up a little song: 'Ding dong bell, Donna's in the well'.

Anyway, my concern wasn't about me, it was about trying to find a way to help the little children in the refugee camp. They all had blank eyes that said nothing. Their stomachs were empty but hugely extended from malnutrition. The littlest babies were passed around to any mother who could share milk from her breasts. Toddlers were given milk put into old whisky bottles topped with a rubber nipple. Everyone had runny noses and flies covered every orifice. It was useless to swat them away, there were so many. No one even tried. The latrine for everyone was a deep hole in the ground where the smell made one sick before even approaching.

My main job there was to help with the health and first aid needs of the camp. I cleaned out infected sores, wiped away maggots from any open or wet area on the children and put together classes, hoping to teach the adults the need for basic hygiene. Nothing was a surprise to me. I understood this world. My job description became more inclusive as I began to help out at the one and only hospital there in the valley. Actually it wasn't anything we would recognize as a hospital in the States. It was really only a shell of a building with no running water, little medicine, open windows without screens, and no doors. Patients would lie on narrow cots or sometimes on the floor waiting for attention. Along with the sick and dying people there were free roaming chickens, birds and flies everywhere. And oh yes – the 'holy cows' often roamed right into the building too.

Still, everyone did the best they could with what they had. I labeled medicine bottles and organized them. My self-assigned job was to try to organize the waiting patients and to assist the doctors by trying to get the patients ready for exams, etc. Besides the language barrier, the fact that no one had ever seen a doctor or been in a hospital before and the people's modesty when it came to taking off their clothing made this all the more difficult. We also had to work around the caste system. Anytime someone came in who had priority on the ladder of the caste system, everything shifted and we had to start all over again with who's next. Boy, oh boy, oh boy. Trying to get people to take off their clothes so the doctor could examine them was next to impossible. That was a struggle every minute of every day. I laugh now at the only sentence in the Nepali language that I still remember. 'Luga Pu Comous': take off your clothes.

The conditions there were very primitive indeed. One of the most interesting times for me was when I got to go in the operating room and watch them at work. Although the doctors were reasonably well trained, without medicine, decent medical implements or much water or antibiotics, the patients usually still died, mostly from infection. But I loved it when I got to watch surgery. And I was allowed to bring in my camera! I still have those pictures and I still feel a great fascination just looking at them. I thought it was like seeing how medicine must have been practiced in the 18th century. They prepared someone for surgery by putting the poor soul in a bathtub full of ice, then running a fan on him to help cause hypothermia, which then brought the blood pressure down. That alone could probably kill an otherwise healthy person!

I saw many, many different kinds of surgery – even brain surgery, where the surgeons used a hand-cranked drill and then a saw blade to lift off a section of the skull bone. I have a picture of that drill and can now see that it actually had rust on it. Another reason so few lived, but it was still fascinating to me. Nothing bothered me or made me queasy. The understanding and courage it took for surgery to evolve which now gives so many new chances to live is absolutely awesome. To watch a doctor cut out diseased flesh or sew up a gaping wound was so marvelous to me that it boggled my mind. Medical wonders still fascinate me. Plastic surgery is high on my list of respected professions.

The only time I felt great sorrow was once when I watched a woman during delivery and a little baby girl was born. She was premature. She probably only weighed two and a half pounds or so, but still came into the world breathing and perfect looking in every way. But Kathmandu in 1968 wasn't the time or place for a premature baby to have any chance of survival. The doctors knew this and it seemed that the mother did too. Its fate was simply accepted. I actually accepted it too, until the baby was thrown into a garbage can. The little body was literally tossed into a cold metal trash can as the doctor left the room. I can still remember the dull thump of a tiny body hitting a metal can. The mother simply got dressed, left the room and didn't look back.

I stood frozen to the floor in shock. Soon after they left, I took the baby out of the trash can and laid her on the bed. She was like a perfect little doll. She was soft and warm, with a beautiful sweet face. She had all ten tiny fingers and toes, but there was no movement or sound. I held her and wished someone could have protected her. I wanted her to know that someone cared. I cried for her. She had had one chance at life, and it was extinguished. And I am crying now as I write this from memory. I remember this one little girl without a name that no one knew ever existed. This deeply penetrated my soul. But the reality is that her life wasn't to be. It's a truth that still hurts, but it doesn't change the facts. In the 'real world', life belongs to the survival of the fittest.

Despite the conditions and all its consequences, my memories of that time in Nepal have held a special place in my heart. I felt like it took me back to a simpler time when we were all a part of the natural selection of living. We were all doing our best to survive in the short time we are given on earth. Every little change and advancement given to them was a discovery met with excitement from almost everyone. I liked it there. I never went into culture shock. I miss the people. I miss the children's smile when they saw me come each day. I miss the adults, who had no fear or anxiety. I miss the simple way they accepted each other and shared what little they had. Life was bitter-sweet.

But what I really miss most about Kathmandu are the mountains. They are so majestic, and when a full moon reflects on their snowy peaks, they light up the night. During the day they reach high into the sky and their pure, untouched beauty becomes an indistinguishable part of the surrounding clouds. Those mountains were an inspiration to me. 'Over these things I could not see; These were the things that bounded me' (Edna St. Vincent Millais). It was as if nature wanted to help protect this tiny land by surrounding it with the mighty arms of love and beauty. I miss those mountains.

I also miss helping people who really needed help and who smiled with hope and gratitude. Oh, that was so very long ago. I never did go back to Nepal. I hear it has changed much from the time I was there. I hear that there are tourists and trash everywhere, and that even the mountains now have litter on them. I don't think I would want to see Nepal that way. I'll just treasure the time I had and the way it was in a time and place, in my memories.

While I was gone for those three months, I wrote home to Bill quite often. He wrote back a lot too. I also kept in touch with my sister Margaret. She kept most of my letters and I was glad to have them when I started to write this book. Bill always wrote me things about the current news in America. He said he missed me 'a lot', but he was still very non-committal. Sometimes he would send something like a mind teaser puzzle in his letter. I never could figure out those tricky mind questions, but one day I sent him back what I thought would be a puzzle to him. I signed my letter with the letters ICWFYTBMH. Seems pretty easy to figure it out right now, but when I wrote it, I really didn't expect Bill to know what it meant, especially since we never talked about a loving each other. Those letters stood for, 'I Can't Wait For You To Be My Husband'.

Bill figured it out! When he answered that letter, he didn't ask what the letters meant. He just wrote back ending his letter by using the same letters but changing the last H. to a W. I couldn't believe it. I wondered if this was his way of proposing to me. Or if I had actually proposed to him first. And did this mean we were engaged? I still didn't even know if I loved Bill or if he loved me.

For the remaining month I was away, our letters to and from each of us went right into discussing how anxious we both were waiting for the time that I would be back home. Of all things, I craved milk. The food was good and hearty there. Mostly we ate goat and chicken. Vegetables were always available. Sometimes we had a bit of fruit or some nuts. Even so I had lost about thirty pounds in three months. Luckily, I never got sick. But during the last few days of my stay in Nepal, I was bitten by some unknown bug which caused an immediate swelling to my arm. I didn't think it was anything too poisonous and just figured that if it got worse, I would take care of it once I got home.

On the flight out of the Kathmandu, I flew on a small parachute plane again. Similar baskets and pots and pans were again mounted on the floor center and there were free roaming chickens too. The cockpit door stayed open and the pilots looked about the same age as I was, so I went up front with them for the whole flight over the mountains. It was hard to distinguish the mountains from the clouds or to know if we were going over them or right into them. The pilot was flirting with me and all I could think of was that he should watch where we were flying. We seemed way too close to the snowy tips of those mountains! It was a little bit scary, but at the same time the most glorious sight I think I'll ever see. Certainly that was what one would say was 'up close and personal'… flying under the clouds and between unending snow-covered peaks!

My flight home had me changing planes in Delhi and again in Hong Kong, where I knew I was heading back into the upscale world. I spent a couple of days seeing Hong Kong again and doing some shopping. I bought a pretty little mini skirt outfit – fashion of the day and luckily I was super thin enough to wear it. No more hairy unshaven legs or tied-up hair in a babushka!

Even though I was gone only three months from my own country, I felt uncomfortable coming home. When I boarded the Pan American International flight, I was seated in first class. I was totally unprepared for the world of comfort and cleanliness. I couldn't get over the white tablecloths. I had forgotten how white white could be.

And then as if by a magic transition, I was being served a multi course delicious hot meal complete with wine and dessert. I felt out of place in this bright, clean new world of 'plenty'. All I wanted was to have more fresh, cold milk. I didn't know how much I had missed milk, and I drank it all the way home.

By now my arm was getting even more painful and very red and swollen. I had a large boil of some sort that looked and felt like it getting bigger by the hour. It was so painful I couldn't even pick up my silverware. We put hot compresses on it most of the flight home but the infection was now spreading up my arm. I knew I should go straight to the hospital when we landed.

Bill met my flight and drove me right to the United Medical Center at the airport. I had blood poisoning going up my arm and the boil had to be lanced and a drainage tube put in. I was super glad that I could trust they had clean needles and antibiotics.

Finally we were on our way home. I remember riding in the car and how it felt motionless as it glided across miles of smooth roads that were all paved. The highways were filled with expensive looking cars of all types. Along the sides of the roads there were unending buildings. Everything was gigantic! There were big buildings and stores and shops everywhere. It was odd that they all looked empty. I couldn't imagine what anyone needed in any one of those stores. Every place we went was filled with an abundance of… things. What did everyone do with them?

Now, fifty years later, I still remember that impression I had when I came back to America. I really didn't feel like I belonged in my own country. Coming home, I definitely had culture shock. I often still look around and I'm amazed at the vastness and wealth that is everywhere in this country. I still don't understand what everyone shops for in all the stores, but I am grateful to have been born in this land of beauty and opportunity. I feel a comfort in knowing I have so many blessings all around me.

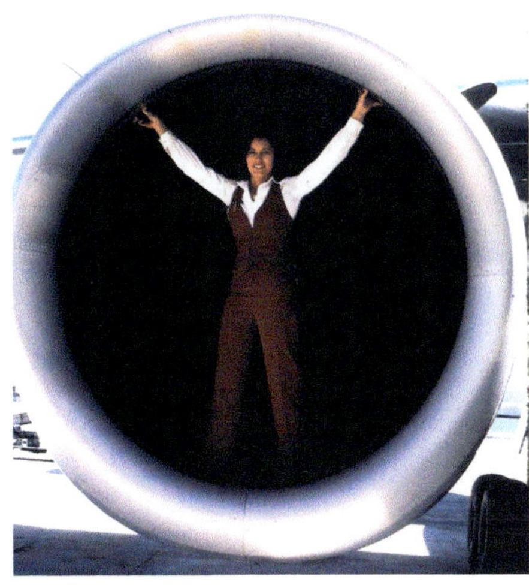

Chapter 5

What's Love Got To Do With It?

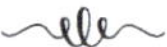

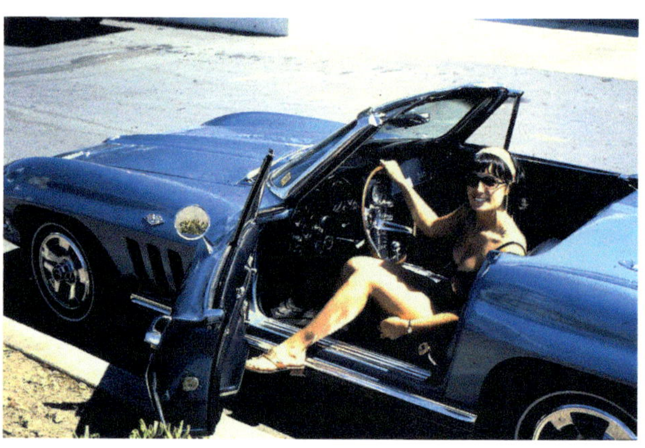

Bill and I immediately started making plans to get married. We were in automatic mode and I still didn't know if either of us was really in love with the other. I knew he wasn't what I imagined as the man who would be my husband some day, but he had a lot of qualities that I admired, the most important one being that he treated me with respect and kindness. I felt he needed me and I thought, sure, why not? Of course in the back of my mind, I suspected that we might get a divorce someday, but he was my chance to get married to a good man. Yes, I am the only woman I know who got married already EXPECTING to get a divorce. I was honest about this with Bill. I remember telling him – in a big run-on sentence – that we could get married and then if we got divorced, we could remain friends and on and on. I only stopped talking when I was surprised at the look of shock on his face.

Bill was from a good family. He didn't have any relatives who were divorced and I'm sure he was thinking this marriage would last forever. I asked if he loved me. He said he had loved me since our third date. Who knew? I didn't. It didn't matter anyway. We went on with the plan to get married. Perhaps we both thought we could change the other or maybe neither of us really wanted to believe the possibilities of it actually not working.

So onward we went – me in fast forward gear quickly planning all the details. I certainly didn't consider a big wedding or fancy gifts, but I still wanted our wedding to be special. Interestingly my first thought was to have the wedding in a small chapel. Maybe it was some sort of inner wish that a religious blessing might give my marriage a fighting chance. I also wanted a pretty dress, a cake and maybe even champagne. And since we both flew for the airlines, I was hoping we would go somewhere for a real honeymoon!

Then I started thinking of who to invite. First I called mom and dad to let them know I decided to get married. Dad's only response was, 'Well if you're not already pregnant, don't have children'. Mom just said they wouldn't be able to come.

Then I called Margaret. She couldn't come either. It was too expensive for her to travel and her husband wouldn't let her. I didn't know where my brother Tony was in those years. My best friend Jackie was in Europe. I hadn't really had time to make good friends in San Francisco. And flying wasn't the kind of job that made you close to your working partner, so I only had one girl friend on my side of the invitation list.

On Bill's side, he invited two friends. All of his family and childhood friends still lived in Pennsylvania. His mother had died when he was only thirteen and even though he was very close to his dad and brother, he didn't have the type of support that got involved with things like weddings. Nor did anyone there have much money for things like traveling across the country. Yes, we did think we would go back east and have a second reception. But why spend money on a wedding dress if no one is at the wedding?

I quickly changed plans and decided to just DO IT. Bill didn't care what or where or who or how we got married. He just didn't want a bunch of fanfare over it.

We knew a judge of the Superior Court and asked him if he would marry us. He said yes, checked his calendar, and told us that he could do it the evening of September 23rd. He asked me where I wanted the ceremony and I told him that I didn't have anything in mind yet, so he graciously offered the use his apartment – outside on the balcony with a view overlooking the lights of San Francisco. And so with three days' notice, it was all in a new planning stage.

The fast change of plans stopped me from shopping for a fancy dress. I simply looked in my closet to find something appropriate to wear. I had a lovely form-fitting off-white dress and coat ensemble. Both pieces had small pearls on the bodice and seemed perfect for the occasion. The only problem was that it was full length and actually was a bit too formal, so I cut off the length and made both pieces shorter. Now I only had to buy some new shoes.

My hair was in electric rollers when Bill rang my doorbell. He gave me the ugliest red and yellow orchid corsage that I had ever seen! Besides not feeling the 'specialness' of the moment, even the flower was a letdown. There was no cake. There were no flowers or decorations. No champagne, and I certainly didn't feel like a pretty bride who was about to get married. We had only four friends meet us for the nuptials. The judge was thoughtful in trying to make our little ceremony as nice as it could be.

As the judge started the usual wedding ritual, he asked me if I would 'Take Bill for richer or better'. I immediately caught his mistake and said 'Absolutely'. Then he realized what he said and apologized and repeated it correctly. 'Would I take Bill for richer or poorer'? I said I liked the first vows better, and we all got a big laugh about that. But believe me, I would be sure to remind Bill that this was in our vows. I got him for richer or better. None of the poorer or worse stuff was going to be for me.

Afterwards, Bill took me to a bar to celebrate. A bar where people smoked and drank, and all I wanted to do was cry. I don't remember if we even made love that night. Deep down I knew this wasn't anything like what I really wanted. I just accepted it and didn't know why. I knew I really didn't have any big dreams about life or marriage as such. I just didn't know that without those dreams, none could ever come true.

Looking back, it was all a big disappointment. We got a few small presents, with one that was unique. It was a beautifully covered book with blank pages. My friend said she had been given something similar when she got married, and had written a journal of her marriage in it every year. I had always liked to write, and I liked the idea of doing the same thing, so I started a journal of our marriage too. I promised myself that—for better or worse—I would write in that journal. And I promised that I would do my best to make a good marriage with Bill. Today I read those entries as a priceless chronology of the person I was so long ago and how our marriage and TIME has continued to change both of us.

In the first few years I wrote about wanting a family someday, and about how we wanted to invest and buy a house as soon as possible. I wrote about thinking I was in love and wanting so much to be a good wife. I also wrote that I saw signs of financial troubles with Pan American but never thought it would mean anything to us. It was an acute observation for a young girl – but how little we knew of what was yet to come. Within that year there were many furloughs in the company. Bill was okay for awhile but got reassigned to fly out of New York. I made it very clear that I didn't want to live anywhere back east. If we moved, it was only with the promise that we'd come back to my beloved city of San Francisco. Neither of us wanted to live in New York, so we decided that perhaps we could live in Virginia and Bill could commute easily enough to New York. Plan in action, I put in my own transfer in to fly out of Washington D.C. I knew it was the best option for our circumstances, but I never did like the east coast. Even so, flying out of New York gave Bill a lot of new and exciting layovers. My new domicile in Washington D.C. had me traveling to new places too. We had a lovely apartment and I immediately settled in planning our future and saving for the hopes of someday buying a house.

Within a few years, we managed to do just that. It's a good feeling to buy a home. We both took pride in giving it our own special touches. I had a lot of experience of hard work from my background, so it was natural and easy for me to take charge of decorating, cooking, cleaning, and working in the yard. I loved everything about our new home and everything about being a wife.

For the most part, life was good. Most of the time, Bill was easy to live with and he often did sweet, romantic things. We were close to his family up in Pennsylvania and got closer to them on frequent visits. Bill loved it there, but I was always ready for the chance to move back to the west coast. My heart was still in San Francisco.

In year four of writing in my journal, I mentioned that Bill was drinking more and that we seemed to disagree more. I wrote that our little romances had almost disappeared. I knew when I married Bill that I was accepting a big problem with his drinking, but I thought I was strong enough to change the situation. I thought if Bill really loved me enough, he would see how destructive this was to our relationship and he would want to change. What I didn't understand then was that liquor is a drug, and that Bill was addicted to it.

I wrote that there were lots of good things in our marriage too. We took vacations and had happy times together. Year six we were blessed with a healthy baby boy. He was born on May 23rd, 1974, on the exact day he was due with only a two-hour labor. We named him Aaron. Wow, there just simply isn't anything in the world that can compare to the joy and responsibility of bringing a new life into the world. Lucky for Bill and me, we both had schedules that allowed us to be home a lot of time. We didn't need child care very often. Bill did his share around the house and was a good daddy to his new son. All my natural responses of love and attention came bursting forth into wanting to give full attention to our new baby. Even in the middle of the night, I would get a wonderful feeling when I heard him cry and could go and hold him. It was a feeling of total completeness.

At the time, neither Bill nor I realized that our sex life was disappearing and that we were forgetting how to hold each other anymore. Part of that is a normal process when parents take on more responsibilities and have less time for each other. And truth is that for us, being sexual never was the best part of our relationship. So we slipped into the cycle of staying so busy that we seldom talked or even had much to say to each other anymore. I was always busy and increasingly tired. Bill was always 'trying to make me happy' and apologizing for getting drunk. It became a routine. I was the bad guy complaining and not feeling loved.

And Bill kept wallowing in denial that he had a problem while all the time getting more and more repressed. In time my hope for security was gone and my 'faith' in Bill almost shattered.

Another year or so passed and I was starting to try and build back some control of my lost spirit. We had lived in Virginia for six years and Pam American was in deeper debt. The idea of Bill ever getting assigned back to the West Coast didn't look like a possibility. We both knew that he could commute to New York from anywhere, and it came down to making another decision. I was ready to go back to San Francisco, and he had a choice to come with me or stay there. After much ado, he agreed we could put the house up for sale and move as soon as possible. To me that meant let's do it tomorrow!

I told Bill I would call a Realtor and get things started. A surprise to both of us, our house sold in three days. Bill had left for a trip and came home to see a SOLD sign on our front lawn. We made a good profit on the house – enough to put a decent down payment on our next home in California. I put in my domicile transfer, it was accepted and we were ready to go.

Home prices in San Francisco were high even back in 1975. We paid $100,000 for an old run-down Spanish house that was basically a fixer-upper. That was a lot of money back then, but it was the only thing we could afford. However, it had charm and I could see that it had great potential. I knew that I had the energy to bring it back to some sort of its earlier glory. I loved that old house. What I didn't think about was that work alone couldn't fix up a house. It took money! There were endless repairs that needed attention.

We immediately began to remodel the kitchen. Six months later it was one of the bathrooms, then a bedroom. One of the bathrooms was so ugly that we closed the door and didn't open it until five years later. Slowly and surely we worked continually on almost every wall, ceiling, window or floor in the whole house. It was a labor of love, but it was also a money pit with no end in sight.

And then almost without time to think, Bill got notice that he was to be furloughed. When this happened it wasn't easy for us financially. We had responsibilities and a lot of expenses for our everyday living. And we had a very big mortgage. But I was still optimistic. I had my job and I knew we would manage. Luckily for us we didn't have much debt and our cars were paid for. We also had some investments and cashed everything in. I picked up more flying and we made ends meet.

Neither of us thought Bill would be furloughed for very long. We just assumed he would get right back with Pan American within six months or a year. In the meantime, he found a flying position with an air ambulance. He was on twenty-four hour call every day he worked with them. The new stress of juggling finances, continual home repairs, a two-year-old needing so much attention and full time flying took its toll on me. I was physically exhausted. Bill and I hardly even saw each other anymore! Our marriage was becoming more like a working partnership.

Still, I couldn't complain much. Bill was always kind to me and never made demands on me. And he certainly pulled his share with the housework and taking care of Aaron. But our marriage did not have the foundation to support our growing financial and emotional needs. He drank more. We argued more. I never did understand how Bill could drink so often and continue to fly, but I give him credit that he knew his limits and didn't cross the line where safety was concerned. Maybe. Maybe he only got drunk once or twice a month – I don't remember. I just know that it was devastating to me every time he picked up a bottle. It frightened me that neither of us could take control of this problem.

Yes, I knew Bill had a drinking addiction when I married him.

But even as I became more aware that he had a serious problem, I still didn't see that it was now becoming MY problem too. It was taking precious years away from my ability to build love and respect for him in our marriage. And now it forced me back into my past life of anger and resentment. Sometimes I'd had all I could take. I didn't have the strength or desire to keep badgering 'poor Bill' about anything. Or try to make him recognize the effect his drinking had on himself and our marriage.

Once we got into a big argument and I remember telling him that I wanted a divorce. He was shocked. He said that he didn't know we even had a problem. He didn't know we had any problems? How could he have missed eight years of my feelings? He was in the same denial with our marriage as he was with his drinking! Could he really be so unaware of what was happening? It was absolutely amazing to me. And whether we believe that our lives have a predetermined destiny or that we make our own paths along the way, my life was not ever meant to be easy or boring.

I was starting to understand that I was now a part of our problems. I stopped 'blaming' Bill for my unhappiness. I recognized that I had different choices and for now, I was choosing to stay married. At this point in our marriage, our son was most important. I never believed that someone should stay married for the sake of a child. And if I had really been miserable, or if Bill had really been a bad person, believe me, I would have had a divorce by now. But it wasn't that way. Bill was still a good man and a kind husband. We still needed each other and our son needed BOTH of us more each day. So I focused on the good that we had together. We both shared equal joy in raising our son. We loved going places and discovering new things from the eyes of a child. Just being a mother helped me discover a deeper and more powerful love inside myself. It really wasn't so bad. Together we worked for a common good. And as proud parents we tried to surround Aaron with a balance of happiness, discipline and security.

Then one day, one day when I was just coming home in the middle of the afternoon from a trip, I saw the car door left open in the driveway. My first reaction was to think a neighbor kid had opened it as a prank. Then I thought there must have been some emergency and Bill had rushed into the house and forgot to close the car door. And then I went inside the house and smelled liquor. Bill had been drinking again. It had now escalated to him hiding his bottles so I wouldn't know how much he had. And when I saw him there, too DRUNK to remember he left the car door open when he got home, too drunk to know he shouldn't have ever been driving in the first place and too drunk to understand he could have killed our child, I was furious! And I knew right then I would not ever trust him again with anything, especially not with my SON.

I didn't know I had such anger inside of me. I really didn't. Now I was ready to explode. All my fears and frustrations came rushing out in an uncontrolled rage. Why was it always me holding life together? Why was it me having to take care of everyone else's lack of responsibility? Why was I the only one putting the pieces together while someone else would come and tear it all apart again? Damn, I was mad. Now I definitely wanted a divorce. That was the final straw.

When things calmed down, we talked about getting a divorce. I was deliberate and without emotion. Let's just separate our assets and do what we had to do, I said. Bill asked me if we could please stay together at least until he got back with Pan American so we wouldn't have to sell the house. I decided that might be best, since I quickly understood the financial loss would hurt me more than him. But it had conditions – that I would take all the control and I would make all the rules. And while we were staying together waiting for this unspecified amount of time to pass, I took off my wedding ring and just told him I was going to start dating again. He could do the same, I didn't care.

I had big talk and big actions, but that still didn't mean it was easy. It wasn't an easy time for either of us. Bill was so remorseful that he'd promise anything in hopes we would just stay together. We went on existing together in a lot of pain, and we each drew inward instead of reaching out for help. Aaron was three years old. Through this rough time, we never forgot he was our main focus and first responsibility. He would be given love and attention no matter who had him or where we were.

Never to have too much time in my life without some kind of crisis, I was on a vacation flight when – we had a HIJACKING.

Actually it was an 'attempted' hijacking, as we never left the ground. And it was in 1977 when people weren't usually killed in the process. Most hijackings back then just had the planes flying to Cuba or something. Anyway I was on a plane as a passenger sitting in first class and I had Aaron with me. We were taking a flight to go visit my sister. The plane was still on the ground while we were waiting for the connecting passengers to board. Aaron was standing in the aisle. I happened to look out the window and see a young man—18 or so—walk toward our aircraft and right up the stairs with a rifle. He had a big three-foot rifle. Now we had security back in those days, so I questioned what I saw – could this be a real rifle? How'd it get through security?

And then the man came right into the plane and stood two feet from Aaron in the aisle. About the same moment, the flight attendant came out of the galley and asked the same question I had asked myself. 'Is that a real rifle?' And he said 'YES' and he raised it and pointed it right into her face. He waved it around and demanded to be taken to Cuba.

I grabbed Aaron from the aisle so fast that he didn't have time to sit down as I flung him into the window seat beside me. He was still standing in the seat during those critical first few seconds, when fear is at its highest and accidents happen. Aaron pointed directly at the man and with big arm gestures, he pointed to the man and yelled out, 'Mommy, that man's bad. He's got a gun!'

As flight crew, we all had emergency training on what to do in a hijacking, but I had never had a rifle aimed three feet in front of me and with my child in danger. And to make matters worse then when a gun is pointed and your child calls the man BAD. I can still remember the feeling of almost fainting as I reacted with lightning speed and shoved Aaron down on the seat while I covered him with my body. I whispered so lowly that I couldn't tell if he could even hear me. I said, 'Don't say a word. Be quiet. Be very, very quiet'.

It was the ultimate moment of fear as I waited to be shot in the back. And I wondered, if I was shot, would it go through my body and hit my son? Would it kill me, or if it went into my spine, would it cripple me for life?

I felt like I had stopped breathing. I was trying to become invisible and just kept waiting... waiting for the sound of a shot. I kept holding Aaron and whispering to him not to say a word and to stay down, stay quiet. And he LISTENED. I stayed over my son for what seemed like an hour, but in reality it was probably only a few minutes.

Major danger over, he didn't shoot us and I slowly started to sit up. Now was the time to use what I had been taught in emergency training. It fascinated me even then how a small child knows real danger. They know it even when there is no pain and no loud voices. Aaron knew this was serious. And I knew I was there to protect him.

This man still had the rifle pointed at the flight attendant and he acted like he was on some kind of drug or something. He swayed and he demanded that the flight attendant go and tell the pilots that he wanted to go to Cuba. I kept my head down but was keenly aware of keeping a watchful eye on him, watching his every single movement or action that might cause things to get worse. I could tell he was scared, and a scared person is a desperate person. I was ready and waiting for my turn to take action. He said he wasn't going to hurt anyone. He said he just wanted to go to Cuba. So I buckled up cautiously, thinking, okay by me. I hadn't been to Cuba yet, so let's go.

The flight attendant did a fantastic job calming the hijacker. She said she had to tell the pilots so we could get extra fuel and everything. He didn't want her to go inside the cockpit and he told her to stay outside and just knock on the door to let them know what was happening. She did - she put her head in for a mere five seconds, just enough time to say, 'We're being hijacked'. The doors weren't locked back then, but as she closed the door, I heard it lock. I knew what the phase one action was for the pilots in a hijacking on the ground: if at all possible, climb out the cockpit window and leave the plane. We laughed in training about the pilots getting off the plane first, but in reality there is a smart reason. Without pilots the plane can't go anywhere and if the plane stays on the ground, it's safer for everyone. Of course it would also mean we were left behind with a madman who held a rifle. And I knew that it was going to be another dangerous time when the flight attendant had to tell the hijacker the truth about this situation. It was scary just thinking what his reaction might be when he found out the plane wasn't going anywhere.

The pilots did exactly as I knew they were trained to do: if given the chance, leave the airplane by way of the cockpit windows. I actually saw them running across the ramp. They alerted airport security and within minutes there were continual communications coming by phone to the flight attendant. I could tell she was being helped with stalling techniques while emergency crews got ready to swarm the aircraft.

It took about 45 minutes, and then came the moment I had been dreading. She had to tell the hijacker that we couldn't really go anywhere because there was no one in the cockpit to fly the plane.

He didn't believe her at first. He said SHOW ME! and moved her up that way with his rifle. I whispered to Aaron again, don't move. Stay down. Don't say a word.

When the man saw that indeed there were no pilots on the plane, he turned around and came right up to me and said, 'Let the women and children off the plane'. I was ready for any chance to go and remembered my own training: 'If you have a chance to leave, take it. A chance for survival, make it'. I was immediately up and halfway out the door with Aaron in my arms, and on the way I grabbed a little old lady in the first row and tried to take her with me. She complained, saying, 'I have to get my bag'. And I said, 'No, you don't need anything, let's go!' I took Aaron in one arm and her in the other and I didn't look back.

Some time later, the hijacking was defused. I really don't know how long it took security to finally apprehended that young man and get the rest of the passengers off the plane, but I often wonder what happened to that kid. Luckily no one was hurt. But he's probably in jail for the rest of his life for doing something stupid. And I thought again of how easily we can ruin our lives and how others pay the price for what stupid people do. And then I wondered, why is it that a person goes to jail – for life – for something like a hijacking when no one is hurt? Or for that matter, even a kidnapping if no one is hurt? And unless someone is killed, why does hijacking demand such a high penalty? Is it because of the extraordinary fear we feel when we might be killed? Is it more frightening for adults to be in fear than it is for a child? What is the penalty for sexual and domestic abuse to a child? Children are half the size of their captors and get threatened by someone five times as strong. Children have no weapons and no place to hide. Children are forced to face their enemies every single day of their lives and in their own home, but there's seldom much of a penalty for their fear. Why is that?

Bill and I both wanted to be good parents, but I loved being a mommy more than anything. I don't think I lived a new childhood through Aaron, but I certainly enjoyed acting like a child when I was with him and shared his joy as we both grew up. I played with him in sports and childhood games. It was as much fun for me as it was for Aaron. I was the one taking him on camping trips, hiking, rafting or skating with him. I was the one signing him up for Space Camp and piano. I embraced all his needs and all his fears. And I treasured his arms around my neck. Aaron taught me the real meaning of love. I understood the words to that sweet little song: 'Love is something that you give away, give away, give away/ Love is something you give away, but it comes right back to you'.

Believe me, Aaron came first in Bill's life too. But Bill wasn't the one taking control or making things happen. We were different in our approach to raising our son, our methods of discipline and even on what we expected for his education. Even so, we just worked things out with a lot of compromising. I discovered that compromising makes no one happy. But we had a good working partnership and we stayed together. For the most part, it worked.

I did start to go out on dates. Being in my thirties and dating again was my way of trying to find out if I 'really' wanted a divorce. I discovered that every part of me was physically, mentally and emotionally begging for attention. I also found out how vulnerable I was. More than ever, I didn't have any answers to my new questions. We both knew we would probably get a divorce. We were just holding on for that elusive 'hope'.

Our new open marriage began to settle, with less hurt and more acceptances. As time passed, I didn't even know if I wanted a divorce anymore. And what did Bill want? Neither of us liked what was happening between us. It was painful to see the look on his face when I left the house, but I did what I thought necessary to change my situation. It was a time that gave both of us more freedom to grow up.

Sometime in that year of painful awareness, Bill decided to fight back.

Chapter 6

Righteous Rage

One day Bill came to me and said the magic words, 'I need help. Please don't leave me and take my son away'. His plea was heartfelt, and his promise to seek help was what I needed to hear. I surprised myself at how quickly I was ready to gamble on another chance for both of us. I wanted to believe it would work. I wanted to change the direction of our marriage and of our life together.

Bill started to go to AA meetings. He didn't like it, but he knew he had no other choices if he wanted me to stay with him. I did my best to support him. I even went to an Al-Anon meeting in hopes to see my own role in this problem.

At my first and only Al Anon meeting, I quickly decided I didn't like anything about it. It started out with a prayer putting our trust in God for what we accepted we 'couldn't do without Him'. I didn't accept the message that we had to lean on someone else or that we couldn't do something without God. All the individual stories were supported with compassion and understanding, but no education was offered about co-dependence or personal responsibility. Anyway, there was a man there who was telling his story about his wife who he met at a bar and their whole marriage of 30 years was totally dysfunctional.

His wife was drunk for days at a time, etc. He went on to say that now after years of excess, she was literally dying from alcoholism. I turned to him and asked, 'If she does die and if you start dating again, would you ever go to a bar to find someone to date'? And he said, 'Yes'. I sat there just looking at him in disbelief. There is no place in my mind where I could ever accept that kind of answer.

I told him that I didn't understand. I told him I would never go near a bar again or date anyone who I even thought might have a drinking or drug problem. The Leader at the meeting immediately broke in and said 'None of us here could know what we might do in that situation'. I strongly answered right back, 'Well I do'. And with that, the Leader said, 'Well then you are the only one in this room who can say that'.

Right then I knew he was right. No one else there understood they were a part of the problem. The only thing I learned from that meeting was that I didn't have one co-dependent cell in my entire body. I still shake my head at how many people never seem to learn from their experiences. No one takes responsibility for themselves. They're all walking around hoping God or someone else will take care of them while they keep wallowing in self pity. Makes me want to scream!

Bill did keep his promise not to drink anymore and we both started going to therapy. Our marriage started changing for the better and I had a newfound desire to love the man I married. We both were finding new ways to communicate. We both wanted to work together for a common goal.

On our first visit to the therapist, I brought in the marriage journal that both Bill and I had written in for ten years. The therapist read it and the first thing he said to Bill was that he noticed he had kept promising to TRY to do better. Then he said, 'Well Bill, trying doesn't work. When are you going to start to DO something'?

Wow, I didn't know that such a little word was so telling of a problem, but that's exactly what the problem was. Stop 'trying' and start 'doing' something to change. I jumped right in to take action, and liked taking on the challenge.

Two years passed and it really did seem like our problems were all in our past. I was happily thinking of us picking up the pieces and putting things together again. But then, Bill stopped going to the AA meetings. And he didn't want to go back to therapy anymore. He was thinking he was okay, and didn't need anymore help. And anyway, he was JUST DOING ALL THIS FOR ME. Another red flag, and this time I knew we had to reach a deeper understanding. I knew he didn't believe he ever really had a problem. So once again, drinking fears penetrated my soul. I was still accepting responsibility alone. Bill was still in denial and his own demon was close to controlling his life again.

And then when I least expected it, I came home from a trip and Bill was drunk again. I remember that I didn't even get upset. I didn't even have a reaction about it. I guess I had expected it to happen and it did. I think when things hit rock bottom; most of us really are alone. It is then that we each can only help ourselves. I never had anyone I could depend on and Bill certainly wasn't there for me either. I wrote in my journal that year that my new word was 'autonomy'.

Bill and I backed away from each other again. Silence was stronger than arguments and Bill knew I was serious about divorcing him. This time he got angry. He said if I divorced him, he would take Aaron away from me. He said he would fight me forever. The thought of losing my son was not an option to me. Period. I never would let that happen, and I knew that Bill wouldn't either, so I simply readjusted my expectations.

I didn't like the choices facing me during that time. Divorce would mean that both of us had too much to lose. So once again, staying together, we just existed without compassion. We were still both involved parents and life went on smoothly for the most part for a few more years. In the process, we were losing the best part of ourselves. Those were not good years for either of us but again, I thought it was my best choice. I think I tried to make the best of my situation. I had a child who needed me. I never lost sight that each moment as a mother had a value and a long-range effect. I did my best. Divorce was not the answer.

Bill was non-committal as ever, probably depressed and just hoping things would get better if he didn't think about them. I was the dominant force as a parent. I was the one who enforced the rules. I was the 'bad guy' who took control of running the house. Bill just didn't have the energy or time to put it all together back then. His part in our family was holding down the finances and showing us the easy-going, peaceful side of life.

Bill and I had few strings attached to our marriage. I dated a few other men once in a while. I was matter-of-fact and candid in all I did. I don't know if Bill ever saw anyone else – he never was up front with his feelings about anything. And I didn't ask anymore questions. I read once that the meaning of 'acceptance' was when you stopped fighting something. Some sort of truth in that. And I didn't fight anymore or try to change Bill. We had a strange silence that allowed us to accept each other from a distance.

Bill stopped drinking – again. And I remember so many of the good things we shared together. Our marriage really wasn't all stress and unhappiness. From hearing what a lot of other marriages were like, I viewed ours as just fine except for the drinking part. We were still both 'good' people who loved our son, and we still needed each other.

Through it all, this was a time when we both tried to make

sure Aaron had a stable home and the security that every child needs. Bill gave him understanding and acceptance. I gave him open arms and kisses, boundaries and bedtime stories. But Aaron always knew, when I was upset, that his daddy was the soft place to fall. I was okay with the way things were. Not my happiest dream-come-true marriage, but okay none the less. My way of loving was with my actions. To me, the word 'love' was not meant to be a noun – it's a verb. Love is an action verb.

Aaron was growing up happy and healthy. He had a wonderful zest for life. He was independent, sensitive and quite capable in everything he tried. He laughed a lot, and had my no-nonsense bottom line thinking. Once we were up in Tahoe on a skiing trip when Aaron was about six and a half years old. His tooth fell out and I made a big deal about it saying the tooth fairy was going to come, etc. Aaron just looked at me like I was crazy and he very matter-of-factually told me that there was no such thing as a tooth fairy. And then he told me there wasn't a big Easter bunny either. And then he paused and said, and there's probably not even a Santa Claus – is there?' He looked right at me and said, 'There's nothing right!' I almost wanted to laugh, but my heart tugged as I visualized the good witch in the Wizard of Oz coming down in a bubble and the bubble popping! The innocence childhood was gone. I knew he had started to question the world and everything around him. I felt it was the bittersweet lessons that we learn as we grow up. Of course we talked about all the deeper meanings of all the holidays, but at that moment I knew that Aaron wasn't afraid to challenge life or to accept reality. There's nothing right? RIGHT. Life is exactly what you make it to be.

I think my writing in the journal during that time showed me that I was growing up a lot in those years too. Year thirteen I wrote in my journal that I was surprisingly relaxed about a problem that was 'so long ago'. Bill and I had a new strength together that allowed us to accept our personal frailties. I had matured into a confident and capable young woman, albeit still with a no- nonsense personality. I like to think that I was strong and loving at the same time. I still couldn't tell if our marriage was going to stay together but I started to see Bill as the man who still kept 'trying' so hard to please me. By the next year, I wrote in my journal that I didn't want a divorce anymore. My choice was made to go forward with him.

We had five pretty good years. Aaron was now at that awkward age of 12 and just plain too good-looking not to go unnoticed by everyone around him. Everything came easy for Aaron. He was smart in school, even though he seldom studied or did any homework. He loved sports and was always actively involved in most of them. He was taking piano lessons, skiing, dirt bike racing and gathering trophies. I loved watching his life so full of joy and opportunity.

But MY life was not meant to be easy for long. The next few years really came down hard on both Bill and me. As we were continuing to upgrade our house, we noticed some major cracks in the foundation. We called in an engineer and were told that the house was in a state of 'disrepair'. That it actually never even had a foundation and was now slipping down the hill. Worse yet, the banks won't loan on a home in disrepair, so even if we sold the house 'as is', the buyer would have to pay in cash. This kind of financial situation could have set us back our whole lives.

When we bought our house, California didn't have the codes or regulations that now were required standards for building or selling a home. We searched for help in every direction and from anyone and everyone who could offer us advice. One of our neighbors said that our insurance might cover the problem. We had always had good insurance, but nothing really happened that I expected the insurance to cover. But we did go to a lawyer and ask what he thought about the situation. He told us he thought we could win a settlement under our earthquake policy. He told us it would probably take a long time but that we should 'go for it'.

It was during this same year that United Airlines went on strike. It was a pilots' strike and I didn't agree with their issues. Plus I needed my paycheck and never forgot that no pilots of any airlines had ever in recorded history supported anyone else in their strikes. So I had no intention of supporting their strike. I crossed the picket lines.

Now if I thought life was hard before the strike, crossing a picket line became one of the most difficult things I have ever done in my life. It was a time filled with unbelievable hate and vicious little people all around me. The same people who talked about respecting freedom and choice. The same people who never figure out that other people's freedom really is only on THEIR terms. It didn't surprise me, but at the same time it was emotionally devastating to stand alone against the world. I have always been ready to accept the price for thinking for myself. I stood strong and did what I had to do. My determination was at full speed forward and I didn't stop to feel sorry for myself.

It was during this time that Bill took a medical exam and the doctors discovered that he had a blockage to his heart. Further tests revealed that he would need triple bypass surgery. If that wasn't bad enough, he would also lose his pilot license.

The stress just kept mounting. Bill was unemployed and his career was over. When it was time to take him to the hospital for his surgery, I truly had no doubt, no doubt whatsoever, that he would be okay. I was so sure that I acted like it was nothing more than a broken bone. I looked at the terror in his eyes as they wheeled him into the operating room and I held his hand and told him, I love you. I'll be here when you come out. I just stood there, physically and emotionally drained. I was so tired of needing to be strong.

This was the very same year I got cancer of the cervix and had to have a hysterectomy. I had no time to even think about myself. Actually I totally forgot I even had cancer until I happened to read over my journal some years later and it reminded when it had happened. 1986 was a very, very hard year. We had been through enough.

That was a very difficult year indeed. The house falling off the foundation, the heart surgery, the loss of a career, my cancer and a strike at United, all in the same year, was just too much. I don't remember how we got through it. All I know is that I felt like I was suffocating and my world was spiraling out of control. It was devastating to realize that no matter how hard you worked and planned and set up assurances, there still was so little security in life. I felt like I was having a breakdown. It wasn't fair! I already had a lifetime of struggle. Would it ever change? I wondered what it was like to believe in a God and actually have the luxury to believe that someone else could take care of things, but the only faith I ever had was the one I held strong in myself.

And anyway, I never forgot that I had the only thing I ever really needed in life – the blessing of a healthy child. I knew that was enough to give me all the strength I needed, to smile, to love, to hope and to keep doing my best to make things better.

Bill was reasonably young when his heart condition was discovered. The surgery went well and he responded quickly to his new exercises and diet regime. He was unemployed for about six months. We had unemployment insurance that helped with finances. During that time he became the 'house husband'. That turned out to be one of the best things that happened in our marriage. Maybe it was that Bill thought he had cheated death, or maybe it was because he was depended upon so much more, but whatever the reason, he was accepting his new responsibilities. I saw a new determination in his eyes as he took his turn at being the man of the house. He had stayed away from drinking, he lost twenty pounds. He was exercising and discovering a whole different way of living. He had more time with Aaron. He had more energy. He had more interests. He took care of cleaning the house, making dinner and totally organizing the home while I worked maximum flying hours. It took a lot of the stress off me to have him home with Aaron, and it was wonderful. It was a healing time for both of us.

I always thought that everyone had a share of good and bad 'luck' in their lives. Some people have more of it than others. A few people actually get an easy ride in life, but it still comes down to the choices we make in our lives that keep us heading in the right or wrong direction. That doesn't mean all choices are easy or that there isn't a price to pay for each and every one of them. It just means you have to decide whether you can afford to pay the price. Bill and I struggled through more than our share of setbacks. I think we usually made good choices, mostly because we had good priorities. We never had the best car or the fanciest clothes among our friends. And we seldom used credit for things we couldn't afford. We just did without vacations every year and the other luxuries we couldn't afford. Still we always managed to put money away for insurance and savings for our future.

And then it finally happened. JACKPOT. One full year later I came home and found a huge floral bouquet on our table. I read the card that was attached and it said, 'WE WON'. I found out that we had won our lawsuit with the home insurance company. Our house was getting a totally new up-to-date foundation. That was the best gift we ever got. Paying for insurance was a 'gamble' that paid off big time for us.

It took nine more months of continual work for the restoration of putting in a foundation to our house. Many other things were being cracked or destroyed and added to the list of disrepair as the process went along. That included most windows, walls, floors and even some of the landscaping. We had to live with the mess of all that remolding for almost a full year, but we got a whole new house when it was finished. Luck had little to do with this windfall. It had to do with us being prepared by having good insurance. Actually to me, that's the definition of 'luck'. It's being prepared to take opportunity when it comes your way. I am blessed. I am blessed. I am blessed.

The next few years were challenging for all of us in different ways. Since Bill couldn't fly anymore, he started a new career in aviation management. He worked more and was paid less for his time. His management style was soft spoken. I could see he was expanding himself and learning a lot more about people as he went along this journey. I learned a lot more too, by watching him. I came to understand that Bill was one of those few men who never needed to be a 'boss'. His strength was in his quiet example. But his solutions to a problem were often still in a bottle.

United merged with Pan American and I had starting flying international trips by now. The timing was perfect for more pay and for being away from the stress of home. It also proved to be another exciting opportunity for me to expand my own horizons and see the world. Oh, I loved flying those International trips! The length of the flights gave us time to read every newspaper or magazine from all over the world. We had time to talk and bond to each other as crew members. We even got to take our breaks in a dark, quiet area with flat beds, pillows and blankets. My usual trips were over the Pacific to Tokyo, Seoul, Hong Kong, Beijing, Sydney, New Zealand and Hawaii. I did some flying into Europe too, but those trips were harder on the body and the people were much more demanding. But jet lag or not, these were wonderful years of discovery.

The way it works is that flight attendants 'bid' for their flights. The time off, the amount of actual flying, the layover points and even the types of airplane are all considered when we chose our monthly flight schedules. Everything is then awarded by seniority. Everyone has a different reason to bid a certain schedule. My main objective was for the layovers. Tokyo was easy and paid the best with increased meal expenses. Seoul was for shopping - pure and simple, because it had anything anyone ever wanted or needed to buy. Packed high to every ceiling of every tiny shop, it was an event while shopping in Seoul just to watch the object you wanted 'appear' like magic from – who knows where? We bought body bags and filled them every trip with bargains galore. We all could tell when a crew member was coming home from Seoul. Customs could too!

Hong Kong and Shanghai were great for shopping too and offered more as scenic destinations. I am still amazed when I think of its transportation system. A million people a day use subways, boats and escalators amd they are all fast and efficient. Hong Kong is unparalleled for a truly International experience. Every kind of food, people, language, building, or event can be seen somewhere in Hong Kong. The city is as high as it is deep with underground levels of transportation, all of it air conditioned, no less! Sometimes we even had five-day layovers, which were like paid vacations. We got to take trips to the Great Wall and Buddha Temples carved into the sides of mountains. Flight crews had great benefits.

Sydney trips were for great seafood, views and harbor tours. London always included a theater experience and if we had a layover in Paris – well, that was for museums and strolling along the Champ Elysee's. I didn't fly to Europe very often, but when

I did, I thoroughly enjoyed the layovers.

Our Hawaiian trips were the easiest and most enjoyable for relaxation. Our uniforms used to be pretty Hawaiian print dresses and we gave flowers to the passengers. We greeted happy passengers and brought them to their vacation paradise. Nowadays most of those flights are like a cattle run. No frills and not even flowers in our hair anymore. But international flying was great and opened a whole new world to me. I liked going to work.

I always knew how blessed we were to live in America, but when you travel as much as I did, and you see first-hand where people don't even have the basics of food and water, you start to understand how unfair the world really is and how politics can control whole cultures. And you see how the people in those cultures have learned to accept the conditions in which they live. Nothing is free in the world. Even basic human rights have a price. No, it's not fair, but it's a reality and if you don't take control of your own situation, someone else will. 'Take control or be controlled'. I read that a long time ago. Oh how true it is.

Aaron was now a teenager and was pushing his limits with both of us. He was a typical teenager with a fierce determination to do anything he wanted to do, whenever he wanted and however he wanted to do it. Of course I was still the disciplinarian, and whenever I put any kind of limits on Aaron, he would fight me. Oh, not literally. Aaron was within good boundaries as a child. He never yelled, cursed or slammed doors. But he sure did find a way to tell me he didn't want me 'controlling' him anymore, not even a little. He would argue if I even tried to ask him a question.

I didn't get much support from Bill in this area. He always felt frustrated in these situations and seldom came up with a solution. He just didn't like confrontation and avoided it at all costs. He had a 'do nothing and they'll grow up just fine' attitude.

Aaron and I were more like each other and both of us wanted it our way, so we bucked heads.

I tried everything – even humor. One time I made a needlepoint sign that said 'My way or the highway', and I posted it on Aaron's bedroom door. The next day I noticed that he had cut out black construction paper strips and covered his door with what he called prison bars. Another time Aaron was talking about how unfair a restriction was that I gave him, so I told him he had a new choice. Instead of restriction, he could write a 500-word essay about punishment. Include an outline of the different types of punishment and detail the pros and cons of each. Here again, I thought it was a brilliant way of teaching a lesson, but Bill thought it was the most stupid thing he ever heard.

Aaron chose to write the essay. He explained verbal punishment, corporal punishment and capital punishment. He said 'capital punishment is the worst because you get killed'.

I actually laughed sometimes at his humor, but he still wasn't getting any slack from mom. I didn't have Bill's support on most of what I did, which gave Aaron a continual reason to stretch his limits. It hurt not to have Bill or Aaron understanding the value of what I was doing. It was devastating to me. Aaron was the soul and foundation that I had always wanted in a family but around this time, he was pulling away from me. I knew he was always independent. I actually had encouraged him to be that way. But around age sixteen, Aaron was totally in his own world where he didn't think he wanted or needed me. I had trusted myself as a good mother, one who surrounded their child and gave him love and opportunity but poof! Just like that, it was all gone. I was pushed out of his life. So when my words become my poems, I wrote.

A bungee For You
No more restrictions to hold you tight
I'll let you go without a fight
But… please understand
Please try and see
How much I need you
To come back to me.

Breaking the ties between a mother and child is hard for most any parent, let alone someone with little else to fall back on. I wanted to cry. I had given my whole life to my son, and I didn't understand what had happened.

I wanted so much to have the emotional support of my husband. I tried to share my feelings with him. I tried to tell him that I needed him to understand me. I needed him to understand himself. We both needed to understand how our past was still affecting our lives. But Bill still wasn't going to admit he had any problems. I desperately tried to make him understand that he was throwing away any chance of us ever bonding and having a happy life together.

I tried everything I could to get a handle on our problems. And suddenly I was vulnerable to every emotion I had ever had ever had as a child. I was totally exposed. I didn't have the strength to fight anymore. My voice would quiver at the slightest confrontation. I felt as if I was having a breakdown. I knew I needed professional help but unlike Bill, I welcomed it. I wanted to understand every single reason about every single thing in my life. I knew it would mean opening old wounds from my past, but it made me want to dig deeper and fight harder for survival.

Bill didn't join me. He remained negative and chose to deny any part of the problems.

I stayed in therapy for a year or so. It confirmed another thing

I had always thought. The only problem that can't be solved is the one that is denied. I was on my own again and I found myself getting angry. I was sick of Bill wallowing in his denial while the rest of the world had to accept responsibilities. I wanted a real marriage and a husband who would fight for it. Once again I thought about divorce. This time I had nothing to stop me. Aaron was old enough and I could simply make the choice to leave Bill.

I wondered how Aaron would react, or if he even knew we had such problems. I wondered if it would be harder for him since he seldom saw his parents fighting. Our home was generally peaceful. We continually shared activities all around him. Everyday life for Aaron was surrounded by two caring parents.

I tried to think of the right way to tell him what was happening. I decided just to be direct and honest. I simply told him that I wanted a divorce from dad. And the minute I finished my sentence, I regretted it. Aaron didn't understand at all. He was totally shocked. He asked, 'Why? Can't you work this out'? He asked if it was his fault. And I said, 'No. It isn't anyone's fault. I just can't make it better anymore'. I needed time to heal.

PART THREE

Chapter 7

The Courage To Heal

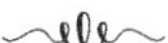

Even though I knew what was going on with my family, it had been several years since I actually saw my mom or dad. I planned a few days to visit with them. Of course I already knew what to expect. When I arrived there were no greetings, no hugs or kisses. The house was filled with an air of apprehension. They still feared me for no sane reason. Dad just stared at me with his pathological distant look. Mom didn't even get up off the couch to say hello. My brother Paul was there as support to them and acted as if he was going to be witness to all the slander he had heard about me. They all chain-smoked and darted looks at each other. I wasn't planning to confront them. I just wanted to understand – why?

No one dared to speak in this awkward silence. I literally could feel the paranoia all around me. My blood pressure left me cold and shivering. When I had a moment alone with mom, I held her hand and asked her only one question. Why? What did I ever do to cause you such fear? She said, 'Donna, you are like a goddam mirror'. I didn't say anything back to her. And I really didn't understand what she meant at the time. I just had to leave because I was crying so hard I couldn't speak anymore.

And so, with no more questions, it was over. I understood without another word said. I finally understood that their fear never had anything to do with me. It was the reflection of themselves that they saw in that mirror of my eyes. They blamed me for exposing the hate and cruelty that they knew I could see.

I left them that day and felt totally free from their hold. I went back to therapy and now asked new questions. I discovered that there's really only one thing to ever learn in therapy: it all comes down to ourselves. How we deal with life as it's handed to each of us. YOU ARE WHERE YOU WANT TO BE. You come into the world alone and you leave alone. But in between birth and death, your life is what you choose to make of it. No matter how the cards are dealt, it's what you do with them that makes the difference.

I can't fight the world and all its unfairness. I can't make anyone like me, no matter how good I am. I can't change anyone but myself. Many a 'good' person in history had been hated, persecuted, hung, burned at the stake, crucified and/or blamed for someone else s sins. It's nothing new. I accepted it and just continued to work on helping myself get out of this reality. I went to several different therapists. I don't remember any great revelations or help as such, until I started reading and doing research on my own. This was where I found the best solution to my own healing.

I read every self-help book I could find, and finally I came across one that really made a difference. It was a workbook called THE COURAGE TO HEAL. It wasn't really all that hard for me to work through the questions and answer them, because I had worked all my life on those questions. This book was a cognitive type of continual therapy for me. It asked questions relating to every type of abuse and dysfunction. Every chapter gave a clear definition of a certain abuse and then followed it with the obvious effects of that abuse. Our written answers revealed our personal pain and guided the reader to different topics like remembering, coping, confronting, breaking the cycle. The workbook helped me connect my feelings and the need to turn them into actions. Then the answers helped turn my actions into change. The book had a chapter about the consequences of those actions. Things like CONFRONTATION. And could you afford the price?

I read something once that said reading helps you learn, but writing helps you understand. So when one of the first exercises started out by asking that we write about the child within ourselves, I understood why that was important. I just closed my eyes and allowed myself to feel that little girl I knew so long ago. Her name still sounds so grown-up. I wrote and asked her what those first five years were like. I only found one picture of her when she was about two years old. Why are your hands clinched in that picture? I wondered. Why do you look so alone and so angry? Did you ever feel secure as a child? Did you ever have anyone to help you? Did you always have to be so strong? I said, hold my hand Donna. Let's take tiny steps and remember who you were. I'll stay with you. I understand all your fears, because I lived them with you. You were so very brave. Did anyone ever tell you how smart you were or how beautiful you were? Even as a child you made good choices. You always knew how to take care of yourself too. And I know that when you grow up, you will shine Donna. I know that… because I am you. Your fears and pain will become your power to change your life. You will break the cycle. And you will make a difference.

When I finished writing that article I was in a mental trance of sorts. I was rocking back and forth and humming a lullaby, the one that says, 'Hush little baby don't say a word. Momma's going to buy you a mocking bird/ And if that mocking bird don't sing; momma's going to buy you a diamond ring'. With that song, I instantly smiled. I wrote my first poem about that little girl.

D IS FOR DIAMONDS, AND DONNA TOO

D is for diamonds. And Donna too.
A coincidence? Well, maybe to you.
Both started out in deep, dark places
Seldom releasing their radiant faces.
When exposed they are pounded, over and over again
Then violently cut for the pleasure of men.
The work is exhausting. The cost is quite high
Understood only by a certain trained eye.
But then something happens
They sparkle. They shine.
The brilliance is power
It's one of a kind.
Still I can't help questioning
The methods, the pain.
Who gets the power?
Who gets the gain?
Few are given this gift to be
I'm very special. One of them is me.
Yes, as I see, so it's certainly true
'D' is for diamonds. And Donna too.

I stayed in therapy for maybe six more months learning to understand the difference between what I could change and what I couldn't. It was several years later that I really began to understand the full meaning of why mom and dad seemed to hate me so much. I projected my disapproval of who they were.

My very difference told them I might TELL of their secrets. Even being silent was a constant threat to them. They never wanted to look in my eyes because it would mean they would have to admit they played a part in destroying the innocent lives of their children and everything around them. It was their hate, their ignorance and their jealousy. It was their own selves they feared most. I knew it was true, but it still hurt me, way down deep inside.

During this time I was definitely changing and finding peace within myself. Bill started to change too. Whenever we had a disagreement, he would stand up for himself. He was more independent of me and was beginning to take action for what he wanted. I could see how he was making different choices and becoming aware that his choices were influencing his actions. I knew he was finally FIGHTING. Fighting for himself. And now I only needed him to fight for me, too.

I went back to visit mom and dad once more. Mom needed a very serious operation and the doctors said she probably wouldn't make it. My heart was kind, but I knew it would be the last time I would see either of them ever again. After surgery mom was on dialysis. The doctors said that she didn't have more than a few months to live. I stayed with her for a week. Some of the rest of the family had come and were taking turns visiting her. No one knew how to deal with their emotions. When we got together, the usual arguments and blame started up for seemingly no reason. No matter who said what, someone had to make an argument about it. And I was still the scapegoat. Not even knowing our mother was dying was enough to mend the hate and mistrust that had festered in our family for so long.

One night when everyone was out and Margaret was already in bed, I found myself in the unlikely situation of being alone with my father. It was awkward but tender at the same time.

I sensed a rare moment of vulnerability in him. I went over to him. I touched his hand and asked if he wanted to talk. I thought maybe, maybe he might say… something nice. It was just an instant of hope.

But all too quickly the mood changed. He snapped back at my touch and went into a self-defense mode. He said, 'Yes, I want to say something Donna. 'You have always been mean and malicious'. I was literally struck silent. I could only stutter out 'I… I am…' I just left the room and cried myself to sleep. To this day, I can hardly believe he said those words about me.

The following year was bittersweet. I felt an odd sadness in the reality of it all. But once again, my life started to change and things were coming together. I discovered that I could put the shame back on those who blamed me for their own miserable lives. I didn't need to hate them. No one could hurt me unless I let them. I didn't cause anyone's problems and I don't need to take the responsibility for them. And now I understood that I didn't have to be perfect either. I took account of my mistakes. I accepted my lost dreams and unfulfilled desires. I admitted that I was 'where I wanted to be'. I was strong and able to take care of myself. I went forward and simply chose to see things from a beautiful, healing perspective.

My mother died on August 14, 1992. No one was by her side. The doctor said that her last words were that she was going to see her baby in heaven, and to tell Donna that she was sorry. 'ell Donna I'm sorry? It was the same predictable story of her whole life. She had a wasted life of regret. I was sort of surprised at my feelings when I heard she had died. I felt relief – relief without any guilt. It was like I didn't have to beg her to love me anymore. I didn't know what kind of funeral would be planned, but I did know that *I* wouldn't be there.

I told my sister Margaret that I knew there would be chaos if I showed up and it was best for me to stay away. Margaret had always been close to mom and dad but said she wouldn't go to the funeral without me. I tried to tell her she should go but she decided to stand by me. My brother Tony didn't go to the funeral either. He instantly decided to stay with his 'sisters'. And my brother Charlie, who was the latest on the be-damned list, was not allowed to go, even if he wanted to. So he joined us.

We four looked around for a small church that would allow us the privacy to have our own memorial to our mother. We each said a few kind words, then we lit a candle and each of us said goodbye. I am glad that some of my brothers and sisters were with me at that time. We needed each other. It was a closing for all of us and a beginning of us learning how to stand together.

As it turned out, there wasn't a funeral anyway. Mom was cremated and supposedly her ashes scattered outside in the back yard. No ceremony, no church memorial. No support from friends and only dad and three of my brothers and sisters were there. I later found out that one of those sisters had found dad in bed with another woman the very day after mom died. And of course that sister and dad had a big argument. He told her to mind her own business and get the hell out of the house. I felt sorry for all of them there at that time. That even as adults, they had to see that cold hearted lack of respect that our father gave to any of us and now not even to our just dead mother. Rude, hateful comments. He didn't care about anyone. Phew – could you imagine if I had been at that funeral? It chills me to even think of that man!

It was raining the day mom died. I remember it rained big, heavy raindrops that never seemed to stop. It made me think the heavens were crying. And it made me want to put my feeling down on paper again. I wrote a poem on the very day mom died.

The words came to me almost without effort. I titled it 'Rain, Rain, Go Away'.

Today… my mother died.
I just don't understand.
I feel
The way I always did when I tried to hold her hand.
Distance
Somehow it seems to grow.
I never quite could touch her heart
I still don't even know
Why?
The heavens have the answer and cry now from above
For the loss of all mankind
With the absence of love.
I think
She said, I'm sorry – her last words said for me.
Deep within my very soul
I felt us both now free.

It's hard for almost anyone to lose their mother, even when there isn't a loving relationship. Maybe it has more to do with losing the illusion of unconditional love. I think it's a major moment in everyone's life, a time when we all have to finally recognize we are alone and are now forced to grow up.

I went home and continued to finish the workbook on the Courage to Heal. I wrote about FEAR. Fear to even look in the wrong direction. I wrote about REMEMBERING. Every day and every night was filled with terror. I wrote about LOSS. I lost my whole childhood. I lost a carefree belief that someone really cared. I lost seeing people laugh freely. I lost the joy of bonding with my parents and family. I lost the feeling of ever being secure. I lost TRUST. Trust in people. Trust that the good will win over the bad. I lost THE BEST PART OF BEING A HUMAN BEING. It has been monumental for me to catch up on learning how to live and love. I have still had to struggle as an adult to see a different world than that which I knew so well. It is a constant effort for me not to slip back into my past. I will not forget what my parents did to all of us. I will not forgive them. I know they didn't have a lot to work with when they were growing up either. But they did have choices. They chose not to learn and they chose to let it happen.

When I finished writing all the facts as I knew them, it was the final step in healing: CONFRONTATION. Several types of confrontation were suggested. The book reminded the reader that there is always a consequence to pay when one dares to confront an issue. Everyone has a different price to pay, and everyone has a different decision to make as to whether or not to even confront their abuser. For me, I chose to send a copy of my whole workbook composition to everyone who knew or was even remotely friendly with my father. There were never going to be anymore secrets in my life, and I wanted everyone to know it.

I put it all together and the unsuspecting 'letter' was ready to be sent. Several good friends encouraged my decision and gave me support. My sister Margee held me closer to her. My brother Tony, who can't even read, knew what the message was about and has been closer to me ever since. Bill and Aaron stood by me with a new understanding. Everyone I knew and all my family members got a copy. Some relatives wrote back words of kindness. Some answered that I should have left everything in the past. Some chose not to respond at all. Charlene never answered. Joye returned the envelope unopened with hateful words on the outside. Charlie called and said he was with me the whole way. And my brother Paul never bothered to answer.

I doubt my father even gave me the consideration of reading the letter. Of course I didn't get an answer from him either. And yes, I did indeed pay a price for that letter. But I don't regret any part of it and I don't want to ever want to forget it either. It takes courage to heal, but not taking the risk to change things keeps them happening all over again. Abusive cycles have to be broken. And we are all partly responsible if we let it continue. What is the point of anything, if nothing is remembered or learned?

Today most of my brothers and sisters are moving forward with their everyday lives, but some remain victims of their past. My sister Margee was diagnosed as manic depressive. In the past, she considered suicide and was once committed into a mental hospital. She tells me that she would never tell a therapist what she really thinks, because they would put her away again. My brother Tony still cannot read and has suffered untold years of emotional pain. Charlene has been diagnosed with borderline personality disorder. She doesn't believe she really has a problem, but she told me she has cried every day of her life. Joye doesn't talk to me, doesn't believe the stories about mom and dad and still lives her life ignorantly blissful of the reality of our childhood. My brother Charlie is still in and out of prison and on and off drugs. He rarely knows where he is going to sleep at night. And Paul, my youngest brother, doesn't talk to me either. He said none of this happened—to him—so he discredits our story and any of the effects he sees in all of us. And dad… well, he has made peace with himself and has said he has been 'forgiven by God'. He's doing just fine.

Through all of this therapy, Bill and I have settled into a decent marriage and lifestyle. It is just easier than a divorce. We made it work to keep our house and our finances together. Major stresses are subsiding all around us. The house was repaired and filled with love and beauty. Aaron didn't really 'leave' me at all. He just moved out to our guest house and remained happy, healthy, capable and wonderfully independent.

Even though Bill didn't seem to be actively working on our marriage, I did realize that he too, was examining the meaning of life. I could almost see him grasping for that new way of living. I remember once I was surprised when he actively stood up for himself. I could see that he was making new choices, and I could see he was now willing to fight for our marriage and – finally – to fight for me. I could feel his determination to capture all those years we had lost together. I never quite could respect Bill when he didn't take action to control things. It scared me, and I thought it meant that I couldn't depend on him. But now I see that his soft manners were simple disguises. His silence was his independent strength that allowed him to let me shine.

I've always been a no-nonsense, serious kind of person. Carrying the weight of the world, I feel like a crusader who always wanted to make a difference. Personally I don't think we all have to walk in someone else's shoes before we understand where they've been. We simply have to open our eyes and actually take time to see and hear their pain. Pain is pain. Suffering is suffering. Fear is fear. It is a reality all around us. It doesn't matter if it's seeing friends die in war, being treated like a slave or being persecuted for being a certain religion or color, it hurts. No one has a monopoly on the pain they've endured, or their own fears or the abuse they've endured. There is no discrimination in life. It happens to all of us and to to many in every level of society. It doesn't even matter if God is on your side. It only matters how we choose to deal with it dond if we ever learn from it. We can remain a victim, or we can choose to fight to make it better.

I do not blame God for not being there for me when I was a child. I don't harbor hate for evil people. But I definitely have learned a lot from life and I have come to think that many a religious book has done more harm to this world than good. It is in our religious books that we are supposed to learn about loving each other, but only as long as you aren't a Jew, a Muslim or a homosexual. Or heaven forbid, an atheist. It is in our religious books that we are supposed to learn the right way to live. But only ONE way is the right way. And for every 'right' way, something else is seen as wrong. And the 'wrong' way is a new reason for hating and killing.

No, I never did believe in God. However, I do think that most of mankind still needs a God and that a belief in 'goodness' and 'damnation' fill a moral direction. Still, it's scary to me how different cultures choose to believe what they want from their own written testaments. The words that some die defending as the 'true' words of God are just discounted by other religions with their own 'true' words from God. They too die defending them. It never did make any sense to me. And why then do so very few religious people live by the words in the Old Testament? Do they just discount the first words that describe an angry, vengeful God with promises of damnation, fire and brimstone? Perhaps the New Testament should be challenged with that same critical thinking as that of the Old Testament. Yes, the bible does have a lot of wisdom and history. But I can't forget that these great books were written by men—ages ago, and most likely with a political agenda for keeping control of the masses in a time of fear and ignorance.

Our religions have controlled and influenced our thoughts throughout the history of life on earth. Our bibles have condemned free thought and kept us dependent on fear. There is a definite connection with what religious books say and that of our own actions. And there is a connection from what they don't say too. Our ten commandments give us priorities of how we all should live. The first three commandments put an importance on glorifying God above all else. And coveting a neighbor's wife seems to be worth mentioning, while there is no commandment that says that we should take personal responsibility to feed or educate our children. There is no mention of loving animals, or plants, or keeping our earth, water and air free of pollution.

In the name of our loving gods, we hold sacred the right to reproduce in HIS image above all else. But few think of the population explosion that limits the earths' resources and continues to destroy the chance for all other things to live. And the holiest of our books everywhere still teach us of good reasons to fight wars, to hate and to fear for the salvation of our very soul if we dare to question any of it. Many cultures even put God together with guns. We even have songs about killing as we march off to war singing, 'Praise the Lord and Pass the Ammunition'. It's a great foot-stomping song and helps everyone prepare to die because 'God is on our side'.

Our bibles infiltrate everything we do, even when we don't think it does, and the words control us. They tell not to judge others, but when we give up our power to take control and 'judge' others, we avoid the reality that there are EVIL people in life that need to be stopped and pay the penalties – on earth – for their bad deeds. We continue to believe that mankind has a special 'higher right' to live on this earth. But that thinking keeps all other life beneath us and without value. We become superior only onto ourselves. Our very numbers destroy and kill anything that gets in our way without concern or understanding of the greater union of every life and cell on this planet.

We have only to look at a billion years of evolution to learn from nature that nothing is born equal. By the way, the word FAIR is not in any of our good books either. Get over it. Nothing in life is born with equal opportunity and life has never been fair. It is avoiding reality to believe otherwise. Our brains evolve just as our world does. We fight wars because we have evolved with genes that instinctively tell us to fight for survival, fight for our mates, fight for power. Political correctness has us giving up our individual value for being smarter or for working harder or being 'better' at anything when we give others credit for doing nothing. Leveling the playing field brings everything down to the lowest common denominator.

Science is discovering more and more specific genes that determine many of our thoughts and actions. A gene has been discovered that causes our compulsive behavior, aggressive behavior or even the addictive personality traits. We know there is a gene that plays a major role in determining passive and aggressive actions. There's a gene that is responsible for depression and risk-taking. There is one specific gene that triggers over-eating and a gene that dominates paranoid personality disorders. Soon science will probably know there is a gene determining why we 'think' with a politically conservative or liberal point of view. Yes, I think we are born with predetermined codes. Of course, that doesn't mean we can't change and learn as we go through life. It just means genetics is a powerful force.

We already know that we are predetermined to favor one sex over the other, so why not those with a sexual aggression towards children? Pedophiles probably have a genetic basis to do exactly what they do too. And that is the very reason we can't 'rehabilitate' them. As we learn more about how the body and brain cells work, science will have a great dilemma to face. The question will be, what do we do about it? Do we 'zap' the so-called bad genes in favor of protecting the person and society at large? Do we continue to hope that education will win over their brain and bred in new tendencies? And WHO makes those decisions as to what is right and what is wrong, what is good or what is bad? SCARY, but I'm all in favor of science trying to do anything they can to 'design' better humans.

We have the same genetic base code as all living things. We live by the same laws that nature has shown us since the beginning of time. The same law that supposedly God created but few want to accept. Actually it's not a bad way to live. If only we could learn from it. And NO, as a species in general, I don't think we are more special or much smarter than animals. We have only to look around and recognize that much of mankind still hasn't progressed to the basic level of finding food and shelter for themselves. Ignorance and hunger keep people desperate. Fear and desperation make us dangerous – the same as with all animals. 'It's a jungle out there'. It's not a perfect world and I'm not sitting around being passive waiting for someone else to make the decisions. I just know that if we don't take our own control, someone else surely will.

One of the most penetrating statements that I ever read was made by a scientist who concluded that 'the universe we observe has precisely the properties we should expect if there is, at bottom, no design, no purpose, no evil and no good. The world is nothing but blind indifference'.

Chapter 8

Philosophy – Who Needs It?

My son said that when he was six. 'There's nothing, right?' The weak die. The strong survive. The ultimate virtue in life is self-reliance. Period. Back to having a philosophy. I believe there is no right and no wrong in the living of it. Aristotle said it first, and it's one of my favorite sayings. To be sure, always open for a great debate. 'There is no right, and there is no wrong. Only thinking makes it so.' Just like in the kingdom of animals. We exist, we fight for life, for mating, for our offspring and power and then... then we die. I don't believe there is any afterlife. I doubt anyone goes to heaven or inherits the earth.

All animals show off for a mate and vie for a position in life with whatever advantage they may have. Man does the same with money. Whether it be by his car, his wallet or his bragging rights, money buys opportunity. I don't hate the rich for having more than I do. I learn from them. By and large they earned their money and they deserve it. They don't owe it to me or anyone else. The truth is that money buys you choice. It buys you shelter, safety, education, and pleasure. It might even buy you a good defense against murder. But best of all, it can buy you FREEDOM. Peace and freedom cost money. The 'price' is internal vigilance.

Of course, I know we are not all blessed with the brains or the ability to make good decisions. Some simply aren't born with the capacity for higher learning. That's exactly why we aren't really equal. And that's exactly why it's so difficult to help others. Survival of the fittest demands we learn to take care of ourselves. This is an obligation we owe to our progression of our very own species as well as to the survival of the whole universe. It doesn't matter how the rules came to be, they have remained the same since the beginning of time. The strong have power. In mankind, power may mean money, muscle or brains. All of these things might work as well as the next – sometimes. But it's smart to understand the rules and be in the best possible position when we want to succeed or need to protect ourselves.

This brings me to another myth that the holy books teach us and which continue to keep us dependent. The stories are all about how sinful it is to covet money. I never hear any stories where the rich guy is the good one. We seldom are told that the rich man worked hard and saved his money. More often than not, he is viewed as being the selfish person who covets money – and of course, who never shares it. And then it's he who usually steals it from the poor. This belief that continues to be preached to us in bibles and childhood storybooks not only persuades the poor to blame the rich for their problems, but doesn't give credit to those who EARNED their rewards in life. It keeps us from knowing that money is POWER. It can buy us health and it can buy us freedom. It's a good thing to have.

It's a choice to have children when you can or cannot afford them. It's a choice to marry someone who treats you badly. And it's a choice to be homeless instead of accepting the responsibility to take care of yourself. It's your choice to be reckless or take drugs while someone else has to pay the price after you end up in the hospital. And it's your choice to blame others for your misfortunes on others while you choose to remain a victim. Nothing in nature has ever been fair or equal. It's up to you to do nothing, or to get involved to make a change happen. And it's up to you to pay the consequences for your choices.

And the children, always the children, and the innocent are made to suffer the consequences of those who do not take responsibility. Our environment, the animals and the children, all become the victims of those who abuse, those who destroy without the care or understanding of the harm they do to everything around them. It is those who TAKE and don't give back that hurt society the most. My heart goes out to the innocent victims. I was there. I lived under the abuse of irresponsibility. It is what it is. Unfortunately, no one can really help others. We have to want to help ourselves first. Only when we learn that lesson will be have the power to then help others. Life and sharing and giving are the essence of being a better human. I think that the true meaning of being 'spiritual' is to be involved. We are a part of all natural things. Take care and do the best with all the forces of living.

There is a simple beauty in the harsh reality of nature. It works. Being an atheist is somehow regarded as not being compassionate, but I think it's just the opposite. The value of our consciousness is the understanding that we are all a part of the living world. Our species is elevated only because of our brain. We continue to learn and to try and help others or act as God when we abort a child or kill with evil purpose. We have created advanced technology that can save lives and feed the hungry. We can make music and share the gifts of art and education. With increased awareness from computers, the internet, carbon dating, travel and discovered opportunities for all, I am optimistic that mankind might finally be on his way out of the dark ages of blind faith. The age of information is here, and it will change the world faster in the next decade than in the hundreds of years since written literature.

So I've said it from my own point of view. Yes, I think we all have a philosophy about life, even if we don't know what it is. And I think there is a direct connection in one's philosophy with where they end up in life. It goes with the old saying that 'you are where you want to be'. Make the most of today because tomorrow may not come. I can only help others when I help myself first.

Chapter 9

Lessons and Legacies

~elle~

I have always been candid and fast in my thinking. I make a decision, and then if for some reason that decision turns out not to be so wise, I make the best of the situation. I don't use the words 'should have' or 'would have' or 'could have'. They have just never been a part of my vocabulary. And I'm a totally task-oriented person. If it's possible to do it, I'll get the job done. If I want something, I take action to find a way to get it. I have a no-nonsense personality and I consider that an asset. I say what I mean, and I mean what I say. I must admit that tactfulness has never been my best quality. And I learned a long time ago that there's a price to pay for not being 'tactful' enough, but I also learned that being true to myself was more important. It's just what it is. I do my best. I don't feel comfortable with large groups. I don't fit in with small talk and most social settings, even though some would swear that I am often the social belle of the ball. I CAN do it, it's just not my comfort zone.

It seldom crosses my mind to worry about the opinions of others concerning my own life's decisions. My priority never was to win friends or influence people. I find it interesting that a lot of friends see me as a leader, maybe because I am not afraid to speak my mind. Sometimes people seem surprised by things I say and do. I don't know why – maybe because so few others jump in and take control of things. Well, why not me? I have always thought that if the average person can do something, so can I. Truth is, I usually can, and usually I can do it better.

I like to think that those who know me best also know that my optimistic spirit and zest for life are my spirituality. I totally immerse myself in almost everything I do. To me it is the essence of living in happiness, being the best I can be. I like being a pulse of the spinning world around me. So maybe I'm not so politically correct in many ways. I gave up trying to be perfect a long time ago. And I'm sure many people won't agree with some of my points of views, but in the end it's always the same. One to a box.

Funny, that old saying 'Everything changes and yet everything stays the same'. Really, that is the truth. Life is full of situations and challenges. We just have to learn how to use better 'tools' to help ourselves. The truth is that this too is nature's way. I know every living thing will take the course of least resistance. But the price we pay for this is the loss of personal strength and individual power. I can't afford it.

In America, we are given the freedom to make choices. Notwithstanding the little children, there is little excuse – very little excuse – for anyone to be poor, abused or uneducated, or not taking the vast opportunity that we have in this country. (Notice I didn't say it was easy.) Or that everyone would get a fair deal. Remember, life is not fair and the truth is, it will probably never will be easy for the majority of people. Life keeps changing, but does the world really ever change? I am reminded of a saying that I read many years ago. It is attributed to Alexander Tyler, but no one really knows who wrote it. We do know many historians repeat it and use in their history lessons.

A democracy cannot exist as a permanent form of government. It can only exist until the voters discover that they can vote themselves money from the public treasury. From that moment on, the majority always vote for the candidate that promises the most money to them. The result is that democracy collapses over loose fiscal policy. This is followed by a dictatorship.

The average age of the world's great civilizations has been three hundred years. These nations have progressed through the following sequence: from bondage to spiritual faith; from spiritual faith to great courage; from courage to liberty; from liberty to abundance; from abundance to selfishness; from selfishness to complacency; from complacency to apathy; from apathy to dependency; and from dependency back to bondage.

In societies in the world today, most are still directed by chance and circumstance. They might not have the opportunities to change their lives. Most Americans think we are safe, but this is false security. Mass communication and easy travel have made us vulnerable to anyone in any part of the world. By way of the computer and advanced technology, there is unending literature and information available to anyone who wants or needs it. There is no stopping the expansion of mankind's collective intelligence. We have only to want it. The world's only hope is that we take the action needed to apply our new knowledge to the advancement of the world. Our choice is to continue to live with ignorance and fear, or we can hate and continue to just take. Or we can understand reality and start to be responsible for our own lives and the world we share. Actually there really is no choice: take control or be controlled.

Yes, religions have given mankind a reason for living in times of unthinkable suffering, but now as we evolve from a world of the past, we have an opportunity to control ourselves and truly live in peace. I quote: 'Man is ennobled by his own responsibility. Thus the death of a God is not the death of mankind, but its very enhancement'. Amen.

PART FOUR

Chapter 10

And The Beat Goes On

It is only now, some fifty years on, that I have knowledge and understanding of who I am and how my past has affected me. In some ways my past hardships were good in that they taught me valuable lessons. On the other hand they forced me into years of struggle that hindered my highest limits. Bill and I are still married. It amazes me more than anyone that I am the one, in retirement, who lives in a beautiful home, who can afford to travel, who has a happy marriage and who is surrounded by beauty and peace.

I seldom have contact with my brothers or sisters, except for Margaret – she and I are fairly close and speak regularly. Although I always had the best relationship with my oldest sister, I recognized early in life that I was somewhat afraid of her. It is only now that I understand why. She can turn on someone in a minute. She has a compulsive nature and admits that she will say anything she thinks someone else wants to hear. If she doesn't take her meds, I never know when she'll get real nasty and then verbally attack me. She has been divorced twice, lives with her daughter and seems very angry about life. Every now and then she'll go back to therapy, which is always a good thing. When she takes her meds, she is a delight. But still, it's hard for me to trust her.

My brother Tony keeps in touch with everyone in the family. He has had a lot of problems growing up and he never graduated high school. Nonetheless, he's jovial and has made a good living for himself as a mechanic and welder. He was in and out of jail in his younger years and has a record for sexual offenses. I don't think he's involved with the seedier side of life anymore, but then again, I never really knew much about how he lived his earlier life. I only know now – he's doing fine. He makes me smile.

Sister Charlene has always been super liberal. She is still living in the hippy world of the past. She loves being FREE as she calls it. She has a nursing degree but never could put her life together. Her whole world seems to revolve around chaos. Things always spiral out of control and then she finds a way to blame someone else for her problems. Of course she denies it all and finds comfort in being a victim. She has bounced from loving me 'the most' to hating me and not talking to me – again. We are so very, very different. Charlene has a loving heart and means well, but we just don't' have a single thought or action in common.

Sister Joye recently decided to call me out of the blue one day. When I asked her why she had stopped talking to me for seventeen years, all she said is that we should forget it all. Forget the past and let's be sisters again. Like I ever did anything to her to cause her not to talk to me! She is still 'joyfully' in denial about our whole past. She doesn't want to hear anything bad about mom or dad, and she defends both of them to this day. She is the one who sent back my confrontation letter unopened with nasty words on the outside of the envelope. I still have that envelope and until I get an answer or recognition as to why she did it, I'm not getting too close to her either. We speak together maybe once or twice a year, but all communication is superficial.

My brother Charlie passed away in 2011. He was always nice to me but we seldom talked to each other. I didn't pursue getting to know him because I didn't want to be near his problems. His lifestyle literally frightened me. Something I learned in therapy was that if you go into a snake pit, you're going to get bitten. Charlie was always in trouble, in jail, hitting someone, losing jobs and/or into drugs. I stay away from desperate people. Although I hadn't seen him for maybe twenty years, I went back east when I heard he was dying of cancer. He had no teeth, lived in squalor and was surrounded by a frightening element of humanity. It was scary just being there with him. I said goodbye to him and still shake my head in sadness. What a sad and painful life he had.

I don't know much at all about my youngest brother, Paul. Tony mentions him every now and then. It doesn't sound like he progressed far in life and it still sounds like he doesn't want anything to do with me. And so it remains. Different worlds, different realities.

There are no stories of great happiness or financial successes in our family. From what I know, little has changed in any of our personalities since we were born.

In my case, I forgot to write in my journal for the ten years. Those were years when one segment of life didn't necessarily feed upon the other. I think it was also around those years when I just let go of fear. My own mirror might have had more to do with me not trying to be perfect than my brain cells but whatever the reason, I found life getting easier. I didn't try to analyze things so much anymore. I didn't dwell on the past, and seldom did I have time to think of the future either. I just found that TODAY was more important. I liked to think of myself as a kinder person – to myself and to Bill.

It seems like years have passed since I've felt the need to actively fight for myself. I have replaced my anger with a new-found peace. And I have caught myself trusting again. Although I will never forget the force and influence that alcohol had on my life, I am not afraid of Bill's addiction anymore. It has been ten years of his sobriety and we've both learned to take it one day at a time.

On our twenty-fifth wedding anniversary, I went out and bought myself a diamond ring. I remember that it was the first time I really thought 'this marriage is forever'. Oh, I obviously never had a dreamy love-affair kind of marriage, but what I do have is a good person who has chosen to share his life with me. He is a rare man who has been a loving father and faithful husband. He has always been by my side. I think that the forces that allowed each of us to be free enough to grow as an individual are exactly why we are now able to know that we are stronger together. We are still very different and separate people, and maybe we never really 'resolved' the problems we had so long ago. But that's not the point. But we have made a family and a new life of sharing so many years of being together. I smile as I think that of all marriages, mine 'made it'. And the joke is – I never had a pretty wedding dress.

Around that time, I wrote another poem. It's in my box of special memories. New words of my feelings and reflective thoughts of a moment in time. This is 'An Ode to Love'.

I almost let you slip away for what I didn't see
A man of gentle goodness
Who always stood by me.

But too, I really didn't realize
When love had come my way.
All without the special words, you did or didn't say.

And now that all the years we've shared
Have tumbled into one
I feel our time together, has really just begun

Chapter 11

Fearless Crusader

Most of my life has been spent trying to force things to change. They never really do, but little things make can make a big difference. Sometimes life can change just by viewing it from a different perspective, and that alone will take you in a totally different direction. Today, I feel like I live in a different world than the one I knew as a child. I don't see the hardships, the fear or even the lower element of people that were all around me at that time. Life is easy now. I am surrounded by good people. People who are educated, people who enjoy being together with their mates, people who cuddle their children and speak softly when they teach them lessons. People who give back to society.

It's so interesting to me to view life from this new environment. When I was a child, I remember thinking everyone around me was a creep. And it was probably true. We are surrounded by people with a similarity to ourselves. Whether this is a lifestyle connection, an educational or financial one or even an abusive personality, we find comfort in people just like ourselves. I think both Bill and I have moved far away from our past. We are now surrounded by decent people with happy families. Our friends now are people who give to their community, people who travel and who take pride in owning their home.

I suspect none of the people who know me today would ever suspect I didn't have a happy childhood, or that life was ever hard for me. But even if they did know, I think few would understand that my past – as well as Bill's addiction – should not be an embarrassment to either of us. It's part of being a human. Bill took control of his life and turned it around. I did too. And for that, I am most proud.

At one time I thought my life wouldn't be important or have memorable stories like in the world's history books through the ages. But what an explosion of events has happened just in my lifetime! This has been quite an exciting time to be alive. The atomic bomb was dropped the year I was born. One month later, America was gaining military dominance and world power. The whole world has changed so much since WWII. I remember major historical events like when Present Kennedy got shot. Our nation and much of the world grieved at this tragic loss of a great leader. And the awesome moment when the whole world joined together for one 'Giant step for mankind' as we first landed a man on the moon! This was the first event that literally happened out of this world. I watched on television as the Berlin Wall came down. And I was in Hong Kong for the 100-year Handover.

Equal pay for equal work was signed into law while I was a 'stewardess'. Women's liberation has taken hold and with it changes in marriage laws, jobs, responsibilities, birth control, fashion and even abortion. I think the advances in the world of computer technology will give mankind their first real chance to get out of the dark ages. Even the poorest of nations will have opportunity to evolve and understand that they can take control of their lives. It's exciting to think that if there is an end for all we do, it will be for the good achieved by each of us taking action.

Today both Bill and I are retired. We have moved into a beautiful new home in a small town on the central coast of

California. We have a full life of friends, volunteer work, and hobbies. We both remain very active. Bill does long distance bike rides three times a week. He takes care of and manages a big yard, the sprinkler systems, the weed whacking, the gopher and deer control, the tree trimming and the holiday lights. I took up piano for five years and finally made my grand piano a useful piece of furniture. I sing in a great Sweet Adeline chapter and we compete regionally as well as do shows twice a year. We also perform several times throughout the community. It's a full time job being in this chorus. It's almost a requirement that husbands help. And it's a great bonus that most of them do. Like who can ever be a grump if you're surrounded by people who sing?

Painting keeps me busy too. I have been painting in oils for the years now and zoomed fast forward with my creative ability. I'm actually a pretty good artist. Who knew? I've been accepted in a couple of galleries and often display my work at local events. I often sell my work, which gives me great pleasure and almost pays for the hobby. Bill and I also usher at two different theaters. We travel a lot, maybe taking two or three trips a year. The joke now is that it's hard having so much fun. We're always going somewhere or doing something. Our calendar is filled a year in advance. It's exciting. We're both lucky enough to be healthy and have energy to get involved with the world around us. Oh, and my friend Jackie and her husband have moved out west and currently live close by me. She remains my faithful friend.

I give my time to the arts. I give my energy and talent to my family, my chorus, to my friends, my house and yard. I strive to keep learning and improving myself. I gave the world a child who is healthy, independent, capable and loving. I pay enough taxes to help half the nation enjoy the roads, schools and free food that is given to them because I pay more than my share in taxes. It's enough! I don't know what the definition of success is to other people but I know that I AM WHERE I WANT TO BE. My only failure was when I thought I could change someone else.

Many years ago, I read a book of daily horoscopes and the title of my September 12th day was 'The Fearless Crusader'. I smile as I remember thinking that it was so perfectly true. I know, I know, all this horoscope stuff is silly and not scientific, but I like that definition of myself.

Could it be that I was destined to be where I am today? Is fate really random and do any of us really have control over our lives? I like to think we do. I like to think we are rewarded when we do our best. I like to think that democracy is more than an ideal. At this point in my life, I see things changing so fast that I wonder if anyone will ever be able to control anything anymore. With the same advanced technology, one person – one person alone – can change the axis of the world. One person alone can use science to create a genius or find the way to make a million sub-humans to fight our future wars. Very scary, this brave new world to be.

SUCCESS. To me, the definition of this is not measured at the beginning or the end of a person's life but in the journey we each take during our lifetime, overcoming the challenges we are given, taking advantages of the gifts all around us and giving back as much as possible along the way has been the path I've chosen. I feel blessed to have written in a journal for a major part of my marriage. Those middle years of my life were the most formative. Those were the years when I started to understand my past, to grow up and recognize that I could make a difference and direct the life of my future. It was a wild ride most of the way, but my reward today is that I feel blessed. Life is 'as good as it gets'.

Chapter 12

Bloom Where Planted

~ee~

Bloom where planted. When I see myself in art, I see a visual of a single simple flower blooming atop a high garbage pile. It happens. And it stands alone, as I do again, because Bill passed away. I am now a widow.

I don't like that word 'widow'. It sounds so pitiful, so much like I want others to feel my sorrow. I don't announce it but I must admit, right now I think it's noticeable. I fight to stay strong and guide myself on the rest of my journey. It has been a tremendous hit losing someone whose life was entwined with my own for almost fifty years. Actually my whole adult life. I now have only memories and even they don't define me anymore.

Everything changed when Bill died. It's been six months now and I've settled into a different routine that is somewhat comfortable. Some say I'm doing better than most – I think I am. Life goes on and I know I'll be okay. I stay busy – very busy. I seldom give myself time to think about my loss or the time when I was married. When I do stop and think about it all, I smile. I smile remembering the good times we had together since retirement. Oh my, Bill was happy. He had a soft and genuine smile. He stayed active, he bonded with friends and he took pleasure in our home, our yard and all the things most men do around the house. And I think he loved me deeply. I smile knowing that we both found peace and pleasure being together. Life is beautiful. We all get a chance to make the best of our lives and then, no matter how good or how rich or blessed, we all die. It's a bittersweet reality, but I can accept it.

These new days I am going forward grabbing onto every opportunity that comes my way. My heart goes in waves of anticipation of newfound adventures and then bounces to an inner anxiety when I think of the unknown in so many new situations. It's definitely different. I'm older. I'm not so cute anymore. I'm not so confident that I'll find another partner to hold me or that if I do, that we'll have much time together to share the fleeting precious years of passing time. I feel vulnerable and am definitely out of my comfort level. Sometimes I feel lost. But life isn't about existing. It's about being a part of the continual cycle. There is no time to dwell and so much more to do.

It's been seven years since I returned to writing this book. I'm way past the government assigned senior citizen age. And I have had time to accept new challenges facing me in life. The reality of being OLD.

Yes, everything changed again. About six months after Bill died, I did meet Mr. Dance and Romance man. He came into my life at the exact time I needed him. Some said he had a smile that would sweep a woman off her feet. I say it was the kisses that did it for me. I must be honest and say he didn't act like most men I had known. His actions were more like the way men are told they should act – nowadays. You know, a gentler and less macho kind of man. It was a whirlwind romance complete with travel, kisses and lots of dancing. It lasted five years and might have continued into the sunset except for the fact that

Covid came along and stopped the world and most everything in it from going forward. Life does have a way to keep us grounded by the forces of nature.

I decided to sell my big house and move closer to my family in San Diego. That didn't help either. Being apart never was the best for a relationship. We kept calling each other and visiting long distance for two more years. Time and distance took its toll and we both knew we wanted someone closer, someone to hold onto and spend our precious Golden years closer together. We also knew the days were getting less in number each day. We separated with fond memories, each of us knowing it was for the best.

But oh my gosh, another harsh reality to face. This time I feel more alone than ever. Seven years older, moving and starting all over again. This time leaving many friends and the wonderful bonds I had with them. I feel a bit unsteady, with technology making everything harder to do when the promise was that everything would be easier and less expensive. We all know that hasn't happened. I'm still waiting. And still waiting for the next chapter in my life to blossom.

These days, I see myself pretty much the same way most other people say they see me. Knowing very little of my past, they see me living the good life. Never assuming I had any difficulty in life, they almost all say I'm hard to keep up with and that I'm an inspiration. And the beat goes on. Maybe I'll start writing another book, this time about some of the details in my life that now make good stories. If I write down some of my best experiences, it might help me remember them and then I'll have a collection of the moments that are now fading into precious memories.

I've had lots of things happen in my life that make good stories. Good and bad, I've had my share of living life to the fullest. Usually, on my working flights, I had the opportunity to meet a decent number of so-called important people, movie stars, entertainers and elected officials. I actually got invited to the Oscars by a foreign academy winner-to-be.

Coming from a nobody world, my life has spiralled out in many directions. Starting off and going alone to Hong Kong –that was in itself a sign of things to come. Heading off to Kathmandu, sure why not? Since then I've also worked with doctors across borders in Guatemala. Way back when I started my flying career, I also started travelling around the world. I got to climb on the Pyramids– before it became illegal. And I got to walk between all the columns at the Acropolis before they became swamped with tourists. I got to touch Michelangelo's Pietà before it was encased with protective glass. I climbed Half Dome on my 50th birthday – I still love sports and stay active as much as possible. I got to shake hands with the President of the United States and – I actually got a private tour inside Air Force One. Oh yes, I was also put in a jail in Korea for a while. But that's another story in itself. Oh my goodness. Well, then again, maybe I should write something about the love stories and challenges of older people – the unseen people called senior citizens. It would surely have a lot of surprises and guaranteed humor that would be understood by all who are lucky enough to have grown OLD. It could start out with a cliff hanger saying something like 'Who knew – they're not boring in bed'.

What a journey. I would like my book to give inspiration to others who have faced similar challenges in their lives. Hopefully it will be uplifting and leave you with the knowledge and awareness that all of us really do have choices. Life is a challenge to all living things. I hope you will embrace your own story. Living each day to the fullest is the best we can do along our journey. Each day we go forward and face the challenges and opportunities that wind our path and give us the pulse of being a part of the greater good we create. My book isn't about whether you agree or disagree with my choices or opinions. It's about my personal growth. It's simply what I learned along the way that helped me find my way. Not right or wrong – just sharing my story. In the meantime, this is now a good opportunity for me to accept the reality of my situation. Closure with my background, with my youth and with my ability to keep up with the world.

I'll Remember You

When I am gone, I leave my heart. And all the memories too
Of life and love and special times, I've spent with each of you
It was a moment, only one. In all eternity
But nonetheless, for evermore, you were a part of me
Thank you for caring and sharing, each your way
Together life continues and brings forth each new day
I hope when you remember me, your thoughts become a smile
And when you see a flower bloom, you'll stop and stay a while.

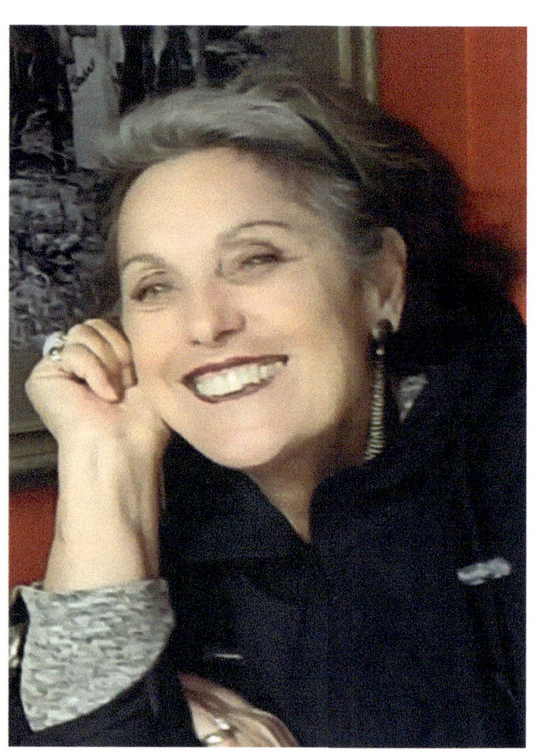

9 7 8 1 8 6 1 5 1 9 9 2 4

finding my wings

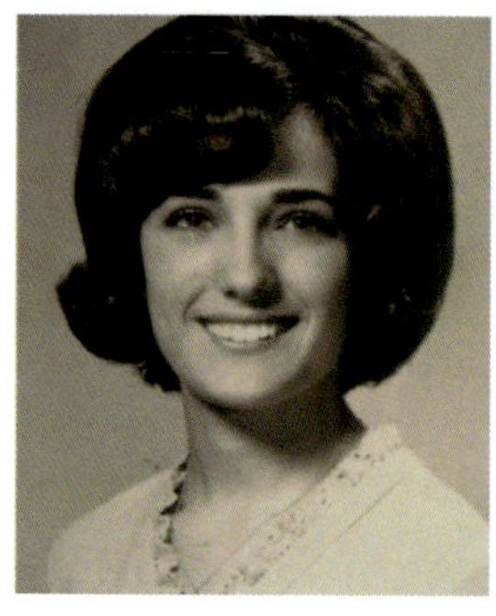

Finding My Wings is the story of the struggle of a brave and insightful little New York girl who had the courage to stand alone and just say NO. After years of coping with life in a dysfunctional, abusive family, she broke free from the abuse and finally, alone in her family, forged a successful career and built a happy marriage. She says: "This story is about the cry for the recognition that we all need and the cry for justice that few of us ever get. It's a common story in all too many homes in the world."

DONNA LONG

ISBN 978-1-86151-992-4

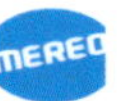

Mereo Books

2nd Floor, 6-8 Dyer Street,
Cirencester, Gloucestershire, GL7 2PF

Tel: 020 3286 8686
Email: info@mereobooks.com
www.memoirsbooks.co.uk
www.mereobooks.com

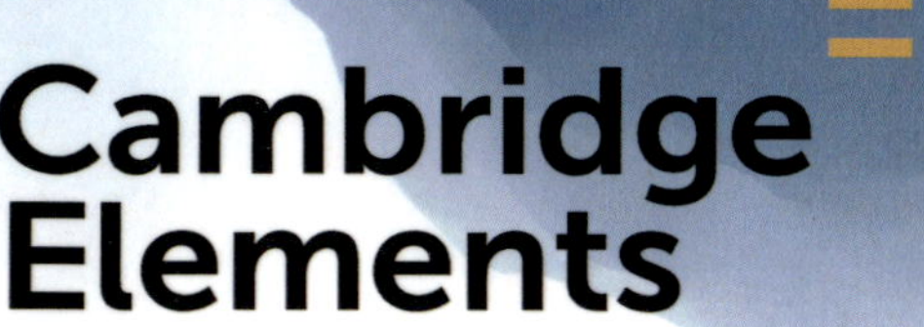

Psychology and Culture

Cultural Psychology and Acculturation

Paweł Boski

ISSN 2515-3986 (online)
ISSN 2515-3943 (print)